Language Course Management

Published in this series
Language Education Management

Language Teaching Competences
Richard Rossner

Language Course Management
Richard Rossner

Language Course Planning (forthcoming 2018)
Brian North, Mila Angelova, Elżbieta Jarosz, Richard Rossner

Language Course Management

Richard Rossner

Great Clarendon Street, Oxford, OX2 6DP, United Kingdom

Oxford University Press is a department of the University of Oxford. It furthers the University's objective of excellence in research, scholarship, and education by publishing worldwide. Oxford is a registered trade mark of Oxford University Press in the UK and in certain other countries

© Oxford University Press 2017

The moral rights of the author have been asserted

First published in 2017

2021 2020 2019 2018 2017

10 9 8 7 6 5 4 3 2 1

No unauthorized photocopying

All rights reserved. No part of this publication may be reproduced, stored in a retrieval system, or transmitted, in any form or by any means, without the prior permission in writing of Oxford University Press, or as expressly permitted by law, by licence or under terms agreed with the appropriate reprographics rights organization. Enquiries concerning reproduction outside the scope of the above should be sent to the ELT Rights Department, Oxford University Press, at the address above

You must not circulate this work in any other form and you must impose this same condition on any acquirer

Links to third party websites are provided by Oxford in good faith and for information only. Oxford disclaims any responsibility for the materials contained in any third party website referenced in this work

ISBN: 978 0 19 440327 6

Printed in China

This book is printed on paper from certified and well-managed sources

ACKNOWLEDGEMENTS

Back cover photograph: Oxford University Press building/David Fisher

The authors and publisher are grateful to those who have given permission to reproduce the following extracts and adaptations of copyright material: p.7 Oxford Dictionaries Online definition of "quality" https://en.oxforddictionaries.com/definition/quality. Reprinted by permission of Oxford University Press. p.61 adapted diagram republished with permission of SAGE Publications Ltd. Books, from *Helping the Client – a Creative Practical Guide* (5th edition), by J. Heron, 2001, permission conveyed through Copyright Clearance Center, Inc. p.82 excerpt and ideas from *Teaching Teachers: Processes and Practices* by Angi Malderez and Martin Wedell © Angi Malderez and Martin Wedell, 2007, Continuum Publishing. Reprinted by permission of Bloomsbury Publishing Plc. p.98 excerpt from 'Observation for training, development or assessment?' by Peter Maingay, in *Explorations in Teacher Training* by Tony Duff (Ed.), 1988, London: Longman. Reprinted by permission of the author and editor. p.169 reference used with permission of The W. Edwards Deming Institute®, for additional information on Dr. Deming's management method, please go to www.deming.org

CONTENTS

Acknowledgements	ix
Introduction	1
PART ONE	3
1 Language course management	4
Introduction	4
Quality	5
Eaquals and quality	7
Roles of managers in language education	8
Who do LCMs serve?	10
Teachers are also managers	11
Conclusion	13
2 Managing the recruitment of new teachers	15
Introduction	15
Recruitment preparation and seeking applications	16
Deciding on the profile of teacher required	16
Preparing other information for applicants	17
Advertising for applicants	20
Selection process	20
Shortlisting	20
Interviewing	22
Appointing	25
Induction and orientation	25
Conclusion	27

PART TWO — 29

3 Working with teachers: management, support, and communication — 30
- Introduction — 30
- The management of the team — 31
  - *People management: some challenges* — 34
  - *Managing serious disagreement and disciplinary problems* — 37
  - *Meetings and other communications* — 40
  - *Written communications with teachers* — 44
- A two-way process — 45
- Conclusion — 46

4 Assessing teachers' development needs — 47
- Introduction — 47
- Balancing teacher development priorities — 47
- The scope of intervention with teachers — 49
- Gathering evidence for development needs — 51
  - *Measures of effectiveness* — 52
  - *Agreeing and recording needs and priorities* — 54
  - *Agreeing and recording steps to meet these needs* — 54
- A flexible approach — 55
- Conclusion — 56

5 Supporting and monitoring teachers' professional development — 57
- Introduction — 57
- Supporting teacher development — 58
  - *Development steps for the whole teaching team* — 59
  - *Development steps for individual teachers* — 62
  - *Mentoring schemes* — 64
  - *Incorporating professional learning into practice* — 66
  - *Reflecting on development* — 68
- Conclusion — 71

6 Observing teachers in the classroom — 73
- Introduction — 73
- Types of observation — 74
  - *Purposes and variables in lesson observation* — 75
- Some guidelines on setting up and running observation schemes — 84
  - *Lesson plans and pre-observation discussion* — 84
  - *Recording or not?* — 85

    During the observation   86
    After the observation – no recording   86
    After the observation – with recording   87
    Consistency   88
  Conclusion   88

PART THREE   89

7 Performance management   90
  Introduction   90
  Appraisal   91
    Purposes, approaches, and systems of performance management   92
  Disciplinary matters and grievances   98
    Disciplinary matters   98
    Grievances   99
  Conclusion   100

8 Course design, needs analysis, and assessment of language learning   101
  Introduction   101
  Course Design   101
    Documentation: curriculum and syllabus   102
  Analysing and determining language students' needs   103
  Quality issues in curriculum and syllabus design   109
    Educational philosophy and values   109
    The purpose and content of syllabuses   110
  Assessment of language learning   113
    Means of assessment   115
  Conclusion   118

9 Managing learning resources and technology   119
  Introduction   119
  Challenges for LCMs in resources management   120
    Managing teaching and learning equipment   127
    Technical support   128
  Blended learning   130
  Conclusion   133

PART FOUR — 135

10 Managing quality: feedback, suggestions, and complaints — 136
Introduction — 136
Total quality management and the PDCA cycle — 136
Internal quality assurance measures — 138
Obtaining feedback from students — 141
Conclusion — 148

11 Managing institutional self-assessment and action planning — 149
Introduction — 149
Developing or selecting standards and indicators — 151
Implementing a systematic review — 152
The bigger picture — 156
Creating an action plan — 157
Adjusting standards and indicators — 159
Conclusion — 159

12 Final considerations — 161
Introduction — 161
The complexity of the LCM's role — 161
The LCM's professional development — 162
Promoting a positive climate — 163
Conclusion — 164

Appendix 1 — 165
Appendix 2 — 173
Appendix 3 — 175
Appendix 4 — 176
Glossary — 179
Website references — 183
References — 186
Index — 189

ACKNOWLEDGEMENTS

This book would have been impossible without the contributions of many, many people to the cumulative work of Eaquals since its foundation in 1991. Several references are made to the Eaquals accreditation standards and the Eaquals Inspection Manual, which was in its 7th version at the time of writing. These documents have evolved gradually since the very first version was produced over 20 years ago. The Eaquals board members, inspectors, directors of accreditation, and members of the accreditation panel who contributed to this work are too numerous to name. Those who successively and collaboratively pulled this work together and turned the documents into useful tools for centres undergoing inspection and for inspectors themselves include: Frank Heyworth, Peter Brown, Ludka Kotarska, Laura Muresan, Maria Matheidesz, Sarah Aitken, Ania Kolbuszewska, Susanna Dammann, and Sue Sheerin. The more recently developed guidelines on blended learning result mainly from the work of a team led by Tim Goodier, and was further shaped by Sue Sheerin.

Other documents referred to in this book include the Eaquals Quality Seminars, notably the second in the series on 'managing the teaching team', which was developed by Martyn Ellis (sponsored by Eurocentres), and, some of the discussion of quality, including the hair salon scenario, has its roots in the first seminar in this series, prepared by Joanna Strange (sponsored by Bell International).

In the chapters on teacher management, performance management, observation, and teacher development, inspiration was drawn from the self-help guidance documents prepared by Jo Raskin, Ania Kolbuszewska, and Joanna Watson, and also from participation in a recent Eaquals project led by Tim Goodier on the recognition of teachers' professional development. In the chapter on curriculum and assessment, there is also reference to the scales of 'plus' levels of the CEFR and other guidance documents developed by Brian North and a project team, and to other work led by Brian and fellow writers of the third book in this series, *Language Course Planning*, Mila Angelova and Elżbieta Jarosz. Reference is also made to the self-help guide on using the European Language Portfolio, developed by Rebecca Blakey. Needless to say, I am grateful to all those who contributed their work to the Eaquals community and many others not mentioned by name.

The many, many teachers and language course managers I have worked with over the years, or held conversations with during Eaquals inspection visits and conferences, are also owed a debt of gratitude. The range of their experiences and concerns along with their good ideas, have all in some way helped to inspire the contents of this book.

Sincere thanks are due to Tim Herdon of Oxford University Press, whose tactful and enlightened guidance helped considerably in the production of the final manuscript of this book.

INTRODUCTION

Background

Language teaching and learning is an ever more crucial part of education worldwide. The days when foreign languages were mainly the pursuit of enthusiasts are gone; today, most policymakers and other **stakeholders** in education have a clear understanding of the power and importance of languages in education and of the cognitive, social, and professional value of learning other languages. The accelerating pace of globalization means that being able to use more than one language has become much more important for further and higher education, as well as for employment. Globalization also brings with it an ever greater and ever more evident need for intercultural understanding and communication to facilitate positive and productive participation in international social groups, and in conversations that span boundaries of language and culture.

Purpose of this series

An abundance of books and other media has been produced for teachers, as well as for **teacher trainers**, but there are very few publications offering practical guidance for those with managerial responsibilities in language education. The three books in the *Language Education Management* series aim to fill this gap by making coherent and practical contributions which draw on the accumulated expertise and resources of **Eaquals**. They each focus on one of three important and interrelated areas of language education:

- the development of language teaching competences
- the management of language education programmes
- the design of curricula and assessment.

About the series

The *Language Education Management* series and the related website materials bring to a wider public the know-how, tools, and guidelines developed within Eaquals and its network of partners. As such, the three books in the series are not intended to be academic studies and do not contain exhaustive overviews of the existing literature. They are designed to provide practical guidance and opportunities for **reflection** for anyone with management, supervisory, and training roles in the field of language education.

There are three guiding principles behind the series. The first is a belief that, since language plays such a crucial role in all education, and more and more education takes place in languages that are not the students' first language (L1), there is a need for foreign language education to be more closely integrated with education across the **curriculum**. The second is that all foreign languages are to be viewed as equal: English may be more widely learned and spoken than other languages, but this does not mean that the methods and approaches used by teachers of English as a foreign language should somehow serve as models for other languages, or that educators and students in English-speaking countries can afford to be less committed to foreign language learning. The third principle is that, while in the areas of language education covered by this series there may be no 'right answers', there is a great deal of good practice to draw on, and a continual need to seek opportunities to further enhance the quality of language education, both in the classroom and through the systems and resources that support teaching and teachers' **professional development**.

With these principles in mind, each book in the series contains background information and practical guidance, as well as tasks which encourage reflection on the ways in which that guidance can best be followed or adapted. Most of the questions in the reflection tasks have no 'right answers', since the best way forward usually depends on the specific characteristics of an educational context. The aim of these tasks is to stimulate readers to think about the suggestions offered in relation to their own experiences and needs.

About this book

Language Course Management, the second book in the series, focuses on the tasks and responsibilities of people who oversee the provision of language courses in different educational contexts, and the deployment, support, and **performance management** of the language teachers who deliver them. *Language Course Management* is intended to be relevant not just to managers working in the field of language education, but to anyone who has management responsibilities related to language programmes, or to programmes which feature foreign languages as well as other subjects, and also to teachers who are considering applying for management or supervisory positions.

Part 1 explores different aspects of quality in language education, discusses the general challenges of the role of **language course manager** (**LCM**), and sets out recommendations for how to manage the **recruitment** of new teachers effectively.

Part 2 focuses on managing language teachers, including how to provide support and development opportunities for them, and how to maintain 'team spirit' and motivation.

Part 3 deals with performance management and the key aspects of supervising course programmes and resources.

Part 4 looks at the LCM's role in assuring the quality of the learning opportunities provided to students by monitoring, developing, and, where possible, enhancing the quality and **effectiveness** of curricula, classroom practice, teaching resources, assessment, and student support.

Additional downloadable resources can be found on the accompanying website. These can be found at: www.oup.com/elt/teacher/lcm

PART ONE

1 LANGUAGE COURSE MANAGEMENT

Introduction

In the literature of language education, there are many books and articles that focus on methodologies and techniques for language teaching and the theories behind them. Indeed, over the last century (see Howatt & Widdowson, 2004) such books and the ideas they put forward have followed one another ever more rapidly. On the other hand, considerably fewer publications tackle the management of language courses. Although there are some notable exceptions (such as White, Hockley, van der Horst Jansen, & Laughner, 2008; Christison & Stoller, 2012), the literature remains relatively sparse.

The same can be said for education in general. Plenty is written and debated about how to teach and support learning, but relatively little is published about how best to manage the work and resources that go into the delivery and processes of education. Yet management has a crucial role to play in what Soini, Pyhältö, & Pietarinen (2010) call 'pedagogical well-being', which they define as the interrelation between the two main goals of education: 'to promote simultaneously high quality learning outcomes and pupils' personal growth and well-being' (p. 208). This pedagogical well-being is critical for both teachers and students in any educational context.

This book is not intended to be an academic study of language course management. Rather, it should be seen as a toolkit to provoke **reflection** and discussion about how best to manage language courses and language teachers to ensure that high-quality and effective language learning opportunities are provided to students, whatever the context. Drawing on the **quality assurance** work of **Eaquals**, the book aims to map out the main challenges in language course management, exploring some of them in depth. The main approach is to raise questions for reflection, and offer suggestions in the knowledge that, given the wide range of contexts and conditions in which language courses are offered and have to be managed, no single solution will be right for them all.

| Activity 1.1 | From your experience as a manager or a teacher in the field of language education, what do you consider to be the three most important areas of language course management that institutions need to concern themselves with? Consider which of these areas can be described as part of 'general management' and which as 'academic management'. |

In answer to this question, you may have identified areas such as **curriculum** design, supervision of teachers, lesson observation, and methods of assessment. These fall into the broad category of 'academic management' and are responsibilities that will be focused on in this book since they directly affect the quality and **effectiveness** of language courses. You may also have identified areas such as financial management, human resources management, management of student enrolment and student records, and management of buildings and equipment. These fall into the even broader category of 'general management', and, whilst they are also important, they are less specifically relevant to language course management, and will therefore not be discussed in detail.

Quality

Language course management, like most management roles, is closely concerned with quality. But what is 'quality'? The word 'quality' is one that is overused and yet it is likely that every person or organization has a unique perception of what 'quality' means. The perception of quality is influenced by the relationship between the needs and expectations of the person or organization receiving goods or services, and the reality of the goods or services provided. In the case of services in particular, the perception of quality is influenced by the way in which the service is delivered as well as by the outcome and effectiveness of the service. Take, for example, the services offered in a hair salon. Usually customers entering a hair salon have some idea of the kind of haircut, style, or other services related to hair that they want. Sometimes the expectations are very clearly defined and explained to the hair stylist, but quite often the hair stylist may be asked for advice. In the customer's mind, the quality of the service is influenced by many factors: not only the manner of the hair stylist, their interaction with the customer, and the skills with which they handle the hair and the hairstyling equipment, but also the surroundings, the music, and so on. But in the end the key criterion will be whether the haircut actually meets or exceeds the customer's expectations, however vague these were, and whether the price meets prior expectations and matches the service provided.

Although this analogy may seem a long way from education, especially public mainstream education, students—even young learners—also have expectations, although these may be 'barely conscious and merely sensed' (see Activity 1.2).

Activity 1.2 Consider the following definitions of 'quality'. Which do you prefer and why? Which do you consider most relevant to educational organizations?

  1 '(Quality is) the standard of something as measured against other things of a similar kind; the degree of excellence of something.' (Oxford Dictionaries; see Website references)
  2 Quality is simply meeting the requirements of the customer.
  3 'In its broadest sense, quality is a degree of excellence: the extent to which something is fit for its purpose. In the narrow sense, product or service quality is defined as conformance with requirement, freedom from defects or contamination,

or simply a degree of customer satisfaction.' (ASQ Quality Glossary; see Website references)
4 'Quality is a customer determination based upon a customer's actual experience with a product or service, measured against his or her requirements – stated or unstated, conscious or merely sensed.' (Feigenbaum, 1986, p. 7)

Education as an experience involves various services, the most prominent being teaching and supporting students' own learning, but also assessment and testing, individual consultations, and recreational activities. Students' expectations as 'customers' are coloured by their earlier experiences of being taught, their desire for educational success, and the expectations of secondary customers, such as their parents/carers or employers. Education is also a trickier service to deliver because, unlike a visit to a hair salon, it continues for a long time—from a few weeks for a short course to 12 years or more in mainstream education—and the impact on the student is mainly in the future, not immediate. Definition 1 in Activity 1.2 may, therefore, be less appropriate in the context of education because comparisons with other services of a similar kind are less easy to make. There are, of course, exceptions. Students do compare the approach and quality of the various teachers they encounter, especially in secondary education, where they may encounter a dozen different teachers in a week. In definition 3, the 'narrow sense' of quality is also not entirely appropriate to education even though much education has to conform to curricula and specific **standards**, not to mention the strictures of public exams, which often seem to drive education. Of the definitions quoted above, definition 4 seems to be the most appropriate for language education, but this makes managing and delivering quality challenging, to say the least.

Much of this book is concerned with quality assurance and the role that LCMs play in trying to ensure that the quality of language education remains high. This role is especially difficult not only because of the complex notion of quality in education, the number of variable factors, and the number of individual 'customers' and 'service providers' involved, but also because the perception of quality is subjective and fluid. Individual students have different ideas and opinions about what, for example, high-quality teaching is. Moreover, the needs and expectations of students today are not the same as they were 10 years ago, and will most likely change again. For instance, compared to earlier periods in the history of language learning, it is now normal in many contexts for students to do coursework with computers or mobile devices both at their institution and outside of class, which has implications for student autonomy from an early age, as well as for the relationship between face-to-face lessons and other learning opportunities. Also, what is seen as 'high quality' when experienced, may not be seen as such high quality in retrospect: it is impossible to know how students will feel about the quality and effectiveness of their education in later life and in mid-career, when the impact or lack of effect of their previous learning experiences is apparent.

Activity 1.3 What kinds of activity can LCMs engage in to assure the quality of the language courses they are responsible for? What tools do they need to carry out these activities?

Common activities include lesson observation of different kinds as well as gathering feedback from students regularly using a variety of methods, such as meetings with **focus groups** and using simple questionnaires. However, quality assurance is much more effective if it is not just a management task but involves others responsible for delivering the services, including teachers, and those with a vested interest, such as parents/carers.

Quality assurance and **quality control**, i.e. the kind of checking that is usually done by outside agencies or 'head office', imply that clear standards are available in the form of criteria or **indicators** that enable both providers of the service and customers to evaluate whether or not the quality of the services provided is as high as was promised in, for example, customer charters.

Quality is closely related to effectiveness. When assessing the quality of education, it is important to consider not only whether the education provided meets the needs and expectations of customers and **stakeholders**, who can include ministries of education, as well as students, parents/carers, and employers, but whether the educational services provided—the teaching, the assessment, the individual support, and so on—are effective in enabling individual students to achieve their potential as individuals and in the job market. Long-term effectiveness is harder to assess because educational institutions typically do not keep track of what happens to ex-students later in life. So, generally, the only evidence available is the results obtained in exams at different stages in education, although the reliability of that evidence depends on the validity and general quality of the exams in question, as well as their practical usefulness in terms of future career development.

The organization of standards, processes, and procedures for assessing quality, and where necessary taking steps to further improve quality and effectiveness in certain areas, can be called quality management which, as will be shown in Part 4, is a key part of the LCM's job, and is also a part of every employee's responsibilities.

Eaquals and quality

Quality in language education is at the heart of the mission of Eaquals, an international organization founded in 1991 by a group of directors of language centres from various parts of Europe. Best described as an international community of practice, Eaquals has developed a quality assurance scheme of its own to enable language centres to check their own standards of quality by undergoing regular **self-assessment** and inspection. For Eaquals and its members, quality is a constant concern that involves all members of staff, not just managers, whose job it is to organize and oversee internal quality systems. Indeed, it concerns anyone who subscribes to the view that there is always an opportunity, indeed a necessity, for language education centres, and educational institutions in general, to seek ways of improving the quality and effectiveness of their courses and other services. Eaquals is not simply concerned with setting quality standards and checking whether these are being met, but also, through its shared resources, its meetings, and the consultative aspects of its accreditation work, with providing ongoing help and support to language education managers, especially those responsible for managing language courses, in defining their own specific approaches to quality management in a wide range of contexts.

Among the twelve areas for which criteria are listed in the *Eaquals Inspection Manual*, six are mainly or partly in the area of language course management, which is the primary responsibility of the LCM but which touches every part of the institution and everyone working in it, as well as the students and those sponsoring them:

- Teaching and learning
- Course design and support systems
- Assessment and certification
- Academic resources
- Quality assurance
- Staff profile and development

The other six areas also involve or affect LCMs directly while not usually being their primary concern:

- Management and administration
- Learning environment
- Client services
- Staff employment terms
- Internal communications
- External communications

As mentioned above, these are sometimes referred to but are not the focus of this book.

Language Course Management and the other titles in the *Language Education Management* series draw on some of the resources that Eaquals has produced and made available to member and would-be member institutions to support ongoing quality management initiatives. The inspection manual, guidelines on **blended learning** and self-assessment documents prepared by Eaquals will be referred to, notably in the chapters on managing courses and teaching and learning resources (Part 3) and those on managing quality internally. Guidelines and training materials produced by Eaquals are drawn on in the chapters on managing language teachers (Part 2), Indeed, as a cofounder of Eaquals and one of its more experienced **inspectors**, the author has, one way or another, drawn on Eaquals work throughout the book.

Roles of managers in language education

This section considers what it means to be an LCM, what they are likely to have among their responsibilities, and who they answer to. A large number of job titles—such as 'Academic Manager', 'Director of Studies', 'Assistant Director of Studies', 'Young Learners Coordinator', 'Elementary Courses Coordinator', and so on—are used in language schools offering courses in one or more foreign languages. People in these jobs often also teach for part of the time. In mainstream primary and secondary schools with a languages department, the terms 'Head of Department', 'Assistant Head of Department', 'Coordinator', and so on are more likely, and in adult and higher education language centres/departments, a range of titles are used depending on the context. However diverse the titles of the jobs and the responsibilities involved, this book will simply use the term '**language course manager**', or 'LCM' for short. As mentioned above, the book does not focus on the whole range of responsibilities that the person or people in charge of a school, language school, college or university department may need to cope with, whether their title is 'Director', 'Head Teacher', 'Operations Manager', 'Dean', or 'Chief Executive', even though sometimes these senior managers also have academic management responsibilities or share these responsibilities with others.

Activity 1.4

Consider the list of duties below adapted from a typical Director of Studies' job advertisement for a school offering mainly part-time language courses aimed at the local community. In your experience:

1 Which four will the post holder spend most time on? Put them in order (1 = most time).
2 Which two will require most care and skill?
3 Which duties might be missing from the list?

a Recruiting new teachers
b Carrying out **induction** of new teachers
c Assigning teachers to part-time and intensive courses, and briefing them
d Creating **syllabuses** and organizing mock testing for public examination courses
e Handling issues relating to individual students, such as unsuitable placement, repeated absence, etc.
f Dealing with any concerns related to teachers' employment
g Syllabus and course design for in-company courses
h Providing feedback to teachers on their courses
i Dealing with problems arising with courses, such as teacher absence, student complaints
j Choosing textbooks for courses
k Carrying out lesson observation
l **Mentoring** teachers
m Helping teachers with methodology, lesson planning, etc.
n Organizing the teachers' conference once per school year

It is perhaps surprising that the duties do not include curriculum development or much about assessment of students' learning. In this case it may be because the curriculum and the main syllabuses, as well as the tests and other assessment procedures, are already in place at the language education centre. If new syllabuses have to be prepared on the basis of the curriculum, or if tests need reviewing and adjusting, this could take a significant amount of time. Even more surprisingly, there is no mention of responsibility for organizing **continuing professional development** (**CPD**) and **in-service training** (**INSET**) workshops for the team, which in most language organizations are regarded as very important responsibilities.

Most LCMs would probably say they spend the majority of their time on assigning teachers to part-time and intensive courses, and briefing them, handling issues relating to individual students, and choosing textbooks for courses (duties c, e, and i in Activity 1.4), although they feel they should spend more time on providing feedback to teachers on their courses, carrying out lesson observations, mentoring/coaching teachers, including helping teachers with methodology, lesson planning, etc. (duties h, k, l, and m), all of which are potential contributors to **teacher development**, as is a CPD programme. These are also the tasks that are likely to require most care, knowledge, and skill, although dealing effectively with issues that concern individual students may also be a highly skilled task. For example, where teachers are worried about a student's attitude, participation, or behaviour, some sort of individual counselling may be necessary rather than the threat of sanctions, but not all institutions employ trained student counsellors so the task falls to the LCM.

As can be seen from the list of duties in Activity 1.4 and this brief discussion, the LCM's role can be very diverse and demanding. The task can, in some ways, be made easier where the person responsible for language course management is assisted by coordinators, assistants, or senior teachers; but this adds another dimension: delegating responsibilities, and ensuring that the management team are dealing effectively with all the areas they need to in a way that is coherent, consistent, and does not duplicate effort. This requires regular communication, monitoring, and good teamwork. These themes are explored at some length in Chapter 3, Chapter 5, and Chapter 7.

Who do LCMs serve?

One of the challenges for people involved in managing language courses is that they are in a role that faces at least two ways. Generally, they are 'middle managers' – that is, not at the level of the Director, school owner, Head Teacher, or Dean. They serve different groups at the same time: students, teachers, and, of course, those top managers. This poses challenges.

Activity 1.5   Chantal is the Director of Studies at a university language centre where there are no other people in course management roles. She planned to spend the day observing lessons, which she has been meaning to do for the last month, but a number of problems have occurred. Her day began with a meeting with her boss, who urgently needs the course programmes for intensive summer courses so that they can be advertised on the university website. Strong enrolments for these courses are crucial for the centre's finances. Then a teacher, Alain, came to see her, upset about some students in his groups who have complained that his teaching is not motivating enough. He is emotional and has asked to have the afternoon off. Finally, three students from a different class came to ask to be moved to a higher class, claiming that the differences in language levels of students in that group are holding them back.

In your opinion, what order of priority should Chantal give to these issues?

Such situations are not uncommon for LCMs, partly due to the fact that they are answerable to various different people in the organization. Arguably, the most important people in any educational institution are the students. However, the problem that the students have brought to Chantal is not one she can easily solve alone. At the very least, she needs to speak to the teacher concerned, who may disagree with the students. Together with the teacher, she may need to review the results of recent assessments. Even if there is some substance in the students' complaint, simply moving the students to a higher class may be impossible for logistical reasons and may also be unwise as other students may ask for similar treatment on the basis of precedent. So, Chantal would need to defer dealing with the problem, for example, by communicating that she will look into it and provide a solution later in the day, or the week.

The problem posed by her boss's urgent request begs other questions: was this on Chantal's list? Had she been given a clear deadline, or was there lack of organization on the Director's part? In either case, the job needs to be done, and requires proper time, so, given her workload, Chantal needs to estimate how long it will take her and agree with her boss the deadline for having the course programme ready, which may mean rearranging other priorities.

The most urgent problem is the upset teacher, Alain. Perhaps if Chantal had been able to do lesson observations earlier in the month as she had planned, the problem might have been avoided. She may have spotted that this teacher was having problems keeping some of his students engaged, and she could have suggested ways in which Alain could change or broaden his approach. Now she needs to get to grips with the immediate difficulty: should she allow Alain to take the afternoon off, which might mean teaching his classes herself if no one else can be found at short notice? Or should she look for a temporary solution that will at least get Alain through the rest of the day, for example, by counselling and coaching him for half an hour? Did students really complain? Should she talk to the students with Alain? These are the kinds of dilemmas that face LCMs on a daily basis.

Teachers are also managers

As mentioned above, a common situation in education is that managers, especially LCMs, were formerly teachers, and often retain some teaching duties alongside their management responsibilities. Many are promoted to their management role without formal training, just some shadowing of and advice from management colleagues. This transition to management is highlighted in the title *From Teacher to Manager* (White et al. 2008). It is worth considering to what extent the skills acquired during teaching experience are relevant when they move to a management role.

Activity 1.6	From your experience as a teacher and/or a student, list three examples of class and lesson management skills that effective teachers need to be competent in. Which is the hardest and why? Which of these management skills are, in your opinion, also useful for managers?

The final question in Activity 1.6 was explored by Fowle (2000) who, at the time, was an LCM himself. He conducted a small survey among seven LCMs in Thailand, asking them to indicate which skills, in a list provided by him, were common to both LCMs and teachers. Those at the top of the common list were the following interpersonal skills:

- establishing rapport
- effective listening
- effective communication skills
- monitoring and **appraisal**.

The LCMs were then asked to state which management skills their experience as teachers had most facilitated. While again interpersonal skills featured high on the list, three of the seven participants in each case felt that teaching experience had also helped them with:

- presenting ideas clearly
- motivating people
- coping with the unexpected.

It might have been predicted that other skills on Fowle's list would also have been highlighted, notably:

- time management – teachers are used to working with clear time limitations at lesson level, as well as at weekly or monthly level, depending on their syllabus
- day-to-day planning and long-term planning
- decision-making – teachers usually do this on a small scale, minute by minute in class.

The LCMs who responded to the survey, however, clearly did not see the similarities between the types of decision-making, time management and planning that managers do, on the one hand, and teachers do on the other, or between other parallel skills not included in the list, such as setting up and supervising tasks or organizing resources. Fowle's conclusion was that 'for several key management skills parallels are clearly not found in the role of classroom teacher. These skills need to be systematically developed to ensure that educators become competent all round managers' (Fowle, 2000, p. 18). Indeed, while both roles involve time pressure and juggling priorities, success in the role of LCM requires gradually accumulated experience and, where possible, specialized training. This is often acquired through working with a more experienced manager, although some language teaching organizations, such as International House London and NILE Norwich, now offer management training courses. We will return to this issue in Chapter 12.

Conclusion

The role of LCMs is a complex and sometimes uncomfortable one, and many who are asked to take on such roles, often while continuing with their teaching, find the experience daunting at first. Over recent decades, 'management' has acquired an aura of mystique and technical expertise, or high-handed threatening authority, or the making or breaking of organizations, depending on the organization and people being referred to. Yet all of us are managers in one sense or another: at the very least we need to manage our lives which, in the 21st century, is not necessarily an easy task, if it ever was. Many people also have to manage the care and support of other (younger or older) family members or friends, and various other services for them. So, paraphrasing the introduction to *Effective School Management* (Everard, Morris, & Wilson, 2004, p. 3), much of what is said about language course management in this book may appear to be common sense. It is, however, important to think through the key issues relating to this special kind of management and certain scenarios that regularly occur in language teaching institutions with a view to reinforcing the skills, awareness, and preparedness of LCMs, and especially to help those with less experience to deal with the inevitable challenges and opportunities of their roles. The aim is to assist LCMs in meeting their obligations to ensure that the quality of the courses they are responsible for is as high as possible, and that excellent learning opportunities and outcomes are offered to students. The purpose of the following chapters is to pursue this process of thinking through language course management tasks, and to aid the development of relevant skills and know-how.

2 MANAGING THE RECRUITMENT OF NEW TEACHERS

Introduction

In many contexts, recruiting new language teachers is a key task for LCMs. Teacher turnover is a fact of life for most educational organizations, and perhaps language teachers are more likely than other teachers to seek opportunities to work in other countries, at least temporarily, and thus change employment more often. Many institutions, especially private and independent language schools and university language centres, offer intensive language courses at certain times of the year, which means that LCMs have to recruit additional teachers on a temporary basis. In addition, there may be sudden changes in student intake or in individual circumstances that mean one or more additional teachers need to be found. Effective **recruitment** can place a special burden on the LCM's shoulders for a range of reasons:

- it can be last-minute, often due to unavoidable circumstances
- it may be subject to time pressures, since new teachers are often unable to start work immediately
- it is often a task that has to be done alongside other ongoing duties
- getting recruitment wrong can have serious consequences.

This chapter will consider the three stages of recruitment, as shown in Figure 2.1. Although this chapter will look at each stage in the process separately, it has to be remembered that, in successful recruitment, the stages are part of a single coherent process.

Figure 2.1 Stages in the selection of new teachers

Recruitment preparation and seeking applications

Deciding on the profile of teacher required

The preparation stage, like all of the stages in Figure 2.1, is important and should not be rushed. It requires a lot of thought on the part of the LCM, who may also need to consult with others in the organization, such as the Director or the person in charge of human resources, to ensure that they are looking for the right person for the job.

Activity 2.1

Consider the two situations below. If you were an LCM in these institutions, what kind of teachers would you be seeking to appoint? What specific experience would the teachers appointed need to have in each case? Use the 'qualifications and training' section of the **European Profiling Grid** (**EPG**) in Appendix 1 to help you decide the preferred profile of the teachers to be appointed to these positions.

Institution A is a school in Buenos Aires that teaches English to young adults and to children aged 6 to 14 (part-time courses after school and on Saturdays). They now have a new two-year contract to teach bank employees off-site at the bank's premises in the mornings between 8 and 11 am. Most employees need general English, but some require specialist skills in English for finance, and also need to be able to write and give presentations in English. The LCM needs two additional teachers to cover this contract, but also needs to deploy them on afternoon and evening courses.

Institution B is a French-medium private secondary school in Switzerland that has a language department that provides English, German, Italian, Spanish, and Chinese classes, as well as French classes for students whose first language is not French. At higher levels, students take the International Baccalaureate (IB) exams. Due to the increase in interest in Spanish, the LCM needs to appoint a new teacher who can teach both lower-level and higher-level students, and also help with French support for international students.

Deciding on the profile of the teachers required is an important but difficult task for the LCM. In addition, knowing how many good applicants there are likely to be is often tricky because this depends on various local factors, as well as the timing of the recruitment. It is therefore important, with their permission, to retain the details of teachers who may have enquired about a job when none was available, and of teachers who have worked for the institution in the past.

In the case of Institution A, the LCM needs to find teachers with experience of working with company employees, even if this experience was not in the banking sector. However, finding teachers who have that experience and who are also experienced with children and teenagers may be a challenge. On the other hand, if they are willing to do both kinds of teaching but don't have recent experience with younger learners, it may be easier to provide mentoring and support in that area than with the in-company courses. Referring to the EPG, which was explored in depth in the first title in this series, *Language Teaching Competences*, an ideal profile for these teachers would be between 2.1 and 3.1 for 'qualifications and training'.

For Institution B, a different kind of flexibility is required, namely between languages. The profile also needs to include experience of teaching at secondary level and preferably up to International Baccalaureate level. In this case, experience as a Spanish teacher may be more important than as a teacher of French: applicants are likely to be native speakers of French, although a native speaker of Spanish with a good command of French may be equally good in this role, provided that they have themselves been through the kinds of experiences with French that international students at the school have to deal with.

Having decided on the ideal profile of the teacher(s) to be recruited, it is possible to draw up a 'person specification' in the form of a simple table, such as the fictitious one for Institution A shown in Figure 2.2. This can be used as a guide not only for potential applicants, but also during the **shortlisting** process.

	Essential	**Desirable**
Qualifications and training	• bachelor's degree in English • initial qualification in teaching English (at least 100 hours)	• master's degree in language teaching or diploma-level teaching qualification
Experience	• at least three years' full-time English language teaching experience • experience of teaching English to company employees, including one-to-one teaching	• experience of teaching English to young learners and adults • experience of course design and materials development
Special skills	• good **ICT** skills	• knowledge of the banking sector and/or economics
Personal qualities	• versatile • energetic • methodical • willing to work flexible hours, including Saturdays	• willing to multi-task • willing to work in a high-pressure environment

Figure 2.2 Person specification for Institution A

Preparing other information for applicants

Activity 2.2 If you were a teacher looking for a job and trying to decide whether to apply to an organization, what other information and documentation, apart from a person specification, would you want to have available before applying? On a sheet of paper, make a list of the information that would be essential to have, and a list of the information that would be desirable, but not essential, in helping you make your decision.

Most teachers thinking of applying to an organization would find it essential to know about the institution, the work involved, and the terms and conditions of the job post. It would be good, therefore, to make this 'essential' information available to prospective applicants by preparing documentation that can be shared online and/or as an email attachment. What to include in this documentation is discussed in more detail below.

1 About the institution

The institution is likely to have a website already, and may also have a printed brochure. However, it is helpful to create an additional document that outlines:

- the ownership, whether public or private, history, and mission of the institution
- whether it is part of a larger group or franchise
- the kinds of courses, especially language courses, offered to students
- the types and numbers of students who attend, and whether these fluctuate or have recently changed
- the numbers of teachers and other staff employed
- whether the institution is certified or accredited by an outside body that checks the quality of its services
- other points that are potentially of interest to applicants – for example, its role in the local community, participation in projects, special awards for good work, and so on.

2 About the work

Like other employees, teachers need to have an exact idea of what is expected of them. It is a good idea to prepare a version of the job description so that before they apply, prospective applicants know about:

- the location of the work and whether it is in one place or spread over different locations, involving travel
- the number of hours per week that they need to be on the institution's premises, the core working hours of the institution and whether they will have to work weekends, and the maximum number of hours they will be teaching
- the kind of teaching they will be doing, such as the age group(s) of students, and whether the course(s) they will be teaching are intensive (10 or more hours per week) or not (2–3 hours per week)
- the curriculum and/or specific syllabuses for each course, whether prescribed coursebooks are used, and how much flexibility teachers have to adapt, supplement, or move away from the curriculum/syllabus
- the type of ICT facilities the institution has, how these are used to support teaching and learning, and whether its use is optional or obligatory

- the type of non-teaching duties that are obligatory, such as attending meetings and workshops, invigilating examinations, supervising extracurricular activities with students, and so on, and how much more time these might involve
- the likelihood of whether the workload varies depending on factors beyond the teacher's control, such as enrolments week by week, and if so, an indication of how much variation is likely.

3 Terms and conditions

This part of the recruitment package needs to be very clear and unambiguous to avoid confusion or, even worse, to avoid applicants accepting a job on the basis of incomplete understanding. It is best to include at least the following:

- The start date of the job, and how long the contract is for – is it a fixed term contract, with a definite start and end date, open-ended, subject to the institution's needs, or permanent? Employment law varies considerably from country to country and category to category, so it is important that employees know in advance what their situation will be and whether there may be opportunities for continuation or progression later on.
- In the case of employees being recruited from outside the country, are visas and/or work permits required and, if so, how will they be organized and paid for?
- The period of notice, including how long employees need to inform the institutions of their intention to resign, and how long the institution needs to give employees to notify them that their contract is ending.
- The period of probation, if any – will there be a period of time at the beginning of the employment when the employees' work is being monitored to check whether it is satisfactory? If so, it is also important to state whether the normal notice period is shorter during these weeks or months (e.g. from one month to one week).
- Information about the salary or, if this depends on the qualifications and experience of employees, the salary range. It is also important to give an indication of what the monthly salary will be after tax and other statutory payments are deducted, especially if employees are moving from one country to another, with different tax rates and/or social security and other contributions.
- Information about other financial benefits, for example variable annual bonuses, 13th-month payments at the end of year, contributions to accommodation and travel for employees moving to a different country, and so on.
- The level of support provided for CPD in the form of workshops and other activities organized by the institutions, and whether financial contributions towards fees for training courses and external conferences are offered.
- Information about other entitlements and the conditions for them. This includes paid holiday entitlement and paid public holidays during the period of the contract, whether holidays have to be taken at certain times, paid sick leave, paternal leave, and whether unpaid leave of absence is possible.

Advertising for applicants

Once all of the above information has been assembled, the job post can be advertised via whatever channels the institution uses, including recruitment websites and social networks. The advertisement should also include information about:

- the position being offered
- the required level of experience and qualifications
- a brief description of the employer institution
- where further information can be found
- what applicants are required to send to the institution
- the deadline for applications
- who they need to be sent to
- whether all applications will be acknowledged and responded to
- when and where interviews will be held.

It is also important to inform current employees about the proposed recruitment, including teachers who work on an occasional, temporary, or part-time basis. Transparency is essential. Part-time or temporary teachers might want to apply for the new post, and teachers might have contacts and former colleagues who would be suitable applicants whom they could forward the advertisement to. Once the details have been made available and applications have been received, the next stage can begin.

Selection process

Shortlisting

Activity 2.3

Consider the curriculum vitae (CV) summaries of four teachers who have applied for the jobs at Institution A (in Activity 2.1). Which, if any, would you shortlist for interview? Why would you shortlist them, and not the other applicants?

1 **Maria-Luisa:**
- bachelor's degree in English (Argentina); certificate in English at C2
- master's degree in applied linguistics (US university); no teaching practice included in the course
- three years' experience teaching English at a private secondary school
- one year weekly private lessons to two company managers

2 **Robert:**
- law degree (UK)
- 120-hour course in teaching English to adults (six hours teaching practice included)
- five years' full- and part-time experience teaching general English to adults in four different countries

3 Virginia:
- master's degree in education (Chile)
- diploma in teaching English as a foreign language
- four years' full-time experience teaching English and Spanish to students on university preparatory courses in the USA
- prior to her master's degree, she worked in a junior position in a large bank in Santiago

4 Andrew:
- bachelor's degree in philosophy (USA)
- 12 years' experience of teaching English in the USA (summer schools), Mexico, Brazil, Paraguay, and Argentina, including two years as a part-time teacher at the head office of a bank in Mendoza, and two years at the Ministry of Commerce in Asunción

Shortlisting is not an easy task, even when much more information than in Activity 2.3 is provided by applicants. The CVs are likely to be quite diverse in both format and the amount of detail they include. The nature of the qualifications and experience gained may also be hard to interpret. In this case, Virginia and, in spite of his lack of formal training, Andrew seem worth shortlisting, and perhaps Maria-Luisa, too.

In all cases where applications are worth following up, additional information is often necessary. Indeed, it is essential when recruiting teachers from abroad because there is a risk that selecting the wrong person will result in extra costs and difficulties for both parties. Some employers try to obtain additional information by providing an application template, or by specifying in the advertisement what details they would like applicants to provide. Institutions may request that, in their written applications, applicants:

- indicate in what ways they match the person specification
- respond to a specific task or scenario, for example, in Activity 2.3, by saying how they would go about planning a course for bank personnel, or for teenagers attending lessons after school
- give an account of the main training and development experiences they have had as teachers since they began their career
- provide details of the classroom methodology and approach to teaching they adopt, for example, with children between the age of 8 and 11, and contrast it with their approach to language training in the corporate sector.

Some applicants may also be willing to provide links to video clips of themselves teaching. This, of course, may offer a more informative insight into the way the teacher works, depending on how 'normal' the teaching situation is. If employers invite this kind of supplement to a job application, it is wise to specify a minimum and maximum length, and any specific aspects of teaching that would be particularly interesting. Applicants may also provide links to their social networking profiles, which may well provide further insights and information about them.

Another aid to finalizing a shortlist is a preliminary short phone conversation with applicants. This can help immediately to confirm whether applicants on the longer shortlist should actually be called in for an interview. The conversation can be quite informal but applicants should nevertheless be warned that they are going to be phoned, by whom, and about what aspect of their application. A simple email message is sufficient, such as:

> *Thank you for your application. Before finalizing the shortlist I would like to talk to you a little about your experience and your approach to teaching. The call won't take longer than 15 minutes. Could you suggest a time when it would be convenient to call and confirm your phone number?*

Once you have spoken to all of the applicants on the longer shortlist, you can let them know whether they will be invited to an interview. Even if they will not be interviewed it is important to keep clear notes as applicants you telephone may expect to be given some feedback on their application, however brief.

Interviewing

When shortlisting is completed, the interview procedure needs to be carefully prepared. Having more than one interviewer present makes it possible to divide up each interview and, more importantly, enables the interviewers to compare impressions and follow up each other's questions. Either way, it is worth preparing an interview script in the form of a set of topics and questions that will explore each interviewee's application in more detail, and elicit key information about their attitudes and skills. Interview scripts are likely to fall into the following sections:

- reasons for the application
- experience and background
- **competence**, knowledge, training, and qualifications
- attitudes and values in relation to the job and the context
- formalities, such as the notice period of the applicant's current job, when the applicant can start, their travel expenses, etc.

The order of these sections, especially the last three, may vary from interview to interview. Indeed, in some contexts, for example where there is a recognition agreement between the institution and a trade union, standard interview questions and procedures may be required.

Many interviewers also find it valuable to include one or more teaching- and work-related scenarios to which applicants have to provide unprepared responses, in order to assess and compare their reactions and their levels of competence and flexibility, as well as to complement the answers received to questions in other sections. Examples of scenarios might be, for example:

- Two of your students regularly arrive late for class and then disrupt other students' work when they arrive. How would you handle the situation?

- Some students in your class tell you that they want to spend more time focusing on grammar and vocabulary, but you believe that more time is needed on communicative tasks, which most students find useful. How would you manage this situation?

Activity 2.4 You are preparing to interview Virginia and Andrew (from Activity 2.3) for the posts at Institution A (from Activity 2.1). You will be assisted by the Director of the school, who has little recent language teaching experience but is keen to ensure that new teachers fit in with the objectives and ethos of the school. Prepare a script of topics to be covered and one or two sample questions for each interviewee. Then prepare an imaginary teaching scenario or incident to test their reactions.

The interview script for Activity 2.4 may begin with questions about why they have applied for this job, and what attracted them to the institution. This would naturally lead to a discussion about where they are in their careers: are they between jobs, towards the end of a job, or wanting to move to the city for personal reasons, and so on? An exploration of their teaching career could then involve asking the applicants to describe their experience in more detail. In particular, they could be asked about the work they have done in the key areas specified in the job description: working with children and young adults, and with company or, more specifically, bank employees. Key questions could focus on:

- what type of courses applicants have taught: how intensive they were, what level of proficiency the courses were intended to lead to, and the methodology/syllabus, materials, and ICT facilities used
- what type of students applicants have taught: their age, nationality, and the reasons why they were attending courses
- what the applicants have found most rewarding about their recent experience, and which aspects they found most difficult to cope with.

Obtaining this kind of information enables the interviewers to gauge the difference between what applicants have been used to and what they will need to adapt to if appointed, and it can also be an important **indicator** of attitude and commitment to the profession.

The next section of the interview could involve exploring applicants' competence, knowledge, training, and qualifications, including asking what sort of **professional development** they have engaged in, both in terms of opportunities provided by employers as well as self-directed development and peer support. A scenario question would also be helpful here to test the applicants' competence level and skills, and explore in more detail how these were acquired and developed. For example, this could comprise an imaginary situation in which discipline in a class of teenage students begins to decline, making it difficult to teach effectively. Alternatively (or in addition), there could be a scenario about the need to deal with special requests for specialized kinds of teaching and materials, such as company employees in small group courses that go beyond the agreed course programme. It is useful to have more than one scenario prepared. There are, however, advantages in being able to compare the responses of different applicants to the same scenarios.

It is worth noting that some interviewers ask applicants to carry out a self-assessment prior to the interview using, for example, the 'core teaching competences' section of the EPG or a similar instrument. This facilitates a more detailed discussion of the strengths and possible weaker areas that applicants believe they have, and also allows the interviewer to ask for evidence or examples of where given competences have been needed in the past.

The next interview section could focus on professionalism, ethos, the way in which the applicant views their work, and on their career intentions. In Activity 2.4, the Director might want to deal with these issues, asking questions about the applicants' general philosophy regarding language teaching, and the way this relates to the objectives and values of their institution, the advice they would give to friends thinking of going into a language teaching career, what they hope to be doing in five years' time, and so on. These are the kinds of questions that might allow the interviewers and interviewees to engage in discussion about key issues to do with attitudes to the profession and relations with students and colleagues. Again, a scenario question could be used.

The interviews in Activity 2.4 could then be concluded by discussing formalities, such as verifying key information about availability, including start date and whether they are able to work full-time, financial arrangements, etc.

It is important to provide applicants with an opportunity to ask questions. Not only can these sometimes provide insights into their preparedness and motivation, but it is also very important that applicants have a chance to find out more about the culture and general approach of the institution. Some institutions organize for shortlisted applicants to have informal time with, for example, one or more senior teachers, who might show them facilities and be able to answer questions from a colleague's point of view.

Interviewing applicants face to face may not be possible, especially when applications arrive from abroad or other distant locations. While not so satisfactory from the applicant's or the interviewers' point of view, interviewing at a distance via Skype or a similar videoconference application is a good alternative.

When interviewing, some organizations use a points system to 'grade' the responses, for example 5 for a very good response, and 1 for an inadequate response. To do this effectively, the written script needs to have spaces to enter these grades against each main point, adding a few additional items to cover general impressions, voice, use of the target language, the types of questions applicants asked, and even how well dressed they are and their body language. If there are two or more interviewers the grades can later be compared and differences of opinion discussed. If there is general agreement, one approach to selection is to add up the grades and consider whether the applicant with the best grades is in fact the most suitable for the job by evaluating what the risks and benefits of offering the job to this person might be.

Often, internal candidates seeking a better position are interviewed alongside external candidates. In such cases, it is important to follow as far as possible the same procedure and questions so that clear comparisons can be made, even though prior knowledge and experience of the internal applicant will obviously influence the decision one way or another. What is certain is that internal applicants will need some kind of feedback on why they were not shortlisted or were not selected after interview. For more senior positions, second interviews are sometimes held, in which certain questions can be focused on in more detail or a prepared task can be discussed. Some organizations like to have an opportunity to observe the applicant teaching before the appointment is finalized, if this can be organized. In such cases, it is important to have a brief list of criteria to refer to during the observation. If after the observation it is decided not to appoint the applicant, feedback needs to be given that is fair and not too discouraging.

Appointing

Before offering the job to someone, it is important to have the contract details finalized, especially hours to be worked, the monthly salary or hourly rate, the holiday entitlement, etc. that will be offered. In the case of appointees coming from abroad, there will need to be information about whether or not help is provided with resettlement, especially accommodation and travel, as well as with visas and work permits. Once this is ready, the successful applicant should be contacted as soon as possible, and the detailed contract and job description sent to them. The offer should be made subject to qualification certificates being presented and positive references being received, so that this can be left until the successful applicant has accepted. It is worth noting here, however, that some institutions check qualification certificates and ask for details of referees at interview to speed up this process.

The selected applicant(s) need to be asked to respond to the offer within a clearly defined time limit. Having documents in electronic form that can be signed and returned by email can avoid delays. The wording of such offer letters and contracts needs to be extremely clear, with all the relevant terms and conditions set out in a numbered list so that no misunderstanding is possible. Among the terms and conditions, it should be mentioned what happens in the case of disciplinary action being taken against the teacher, how **grievances** or disagreement between teachers and the employer are dealt with, as well as all the other issues listed in Figure 2.2 (see page 17). Ideally, at least one other good applicant will be held in reserve in case, for some reason, the negotiations with the preferred applicant do not result in an appointment.

Induction and orientation

Once appointments have been made and contracts have been signed, induction is a critical step in the case of teachers recruited from outside the institution. Again, this requires careful planning and some time. An important way of ensuring that the process is comprehensive and efficient is to have standard documents ready in the form of a teachers' handbook and a checklist of points to be covered.

Activity 2.5	Think of a teaching institution where you have worked. Make a list of the key points that would need to be covered when inducting a new teacher (some of these points will be the same as when inducting any new member of staff). Which four points on your list should be given most time?

The topics to be covered will, of course, differ from institution to institution, but many can be seen as essential in any teaching context. Many of the points may have been dealt with superficially in the information sent to applicants, but the following now need in-depth treatment:

- organizational structure, outlining who everyone is and what their main responsibilities are, including whom the teacher should approach first for what kind of assistance
- formalities to be completed in order to become formally employed, e.g. related to tax and social security, and how to get access to facilities such as the computer network
- institutional ownership, the declared mission or purpose, the values which guide the institution
- the institution's clients, especially the different kinds and ages of students who attend courses
- the course structure in detail, the variety of courses offered, the objectives of each course, course length, typical timetables, etc.
- the curriculum, i.e. the overall educational approach and philosophy, the course syllabuses, including the teaching materials used, and the ways in which students' progress and achievement are assessed
- the premises where teachers work, including the layout, and, if teachers are expected to work in various places, maps and directions for reaching these
- safety, emergency, and first aid arrangements at these premises, and teachers' responsibilities in these areas
- equipment and additional resources available for use by teachers, and where technical assistance can be obtained
- issues to do with photocopying, such as whether there is a copyright licensing agreement in place at the institution, the need to acknowledge copyright and respect limitations, whether the number of photocopies per student or per class is limited, and so on
- the code of conduct for staff, including disciplinary issues, ways in which absence and illness are to be handled, how staff grievances are dealt with, conduct with students, colleagues, parents/carers and other stakeholders, dress code, etc.
- internal quality assurance and **performance management** arrangements, including the way in which lesson observations are handled, the kinds of feedback gathered from students by the institution, and the appraisal or performance review system

- extracurricular activities for students that teachers are expected to be involved in, including any supervision
- obligatory and voluntary meetings and CPD events, such as workshops, and other opportunities for development provided by the institution
- a 'frequently asked questions' section organized under alphabetical headings, covering the key points listed above, as well as other more detailed or less important issues.

Having a teachers' handbook covering all these areas, which need not be in printed form since electronic versions are easier and cheaper to keep updated and to send out, is important because teachers can read it before their first day and refer to it afterwards. However, face-to-face induction is still necessary. A meeting with a manager to go through key points after having read the handbook not only helps to 'break the ice', but also makes it easier to deal with practical issues, such as timetables, teaching materials, assessment, ICT resources, emergency procedures, and so on.

Many institutions also use a **buddy system** to ensure that new staff members settle in quickly and confidently. That is, a suitable teacher who has worked at the institution for some time and is recognized as a good teacher of the kinds of courses the new teacher will be responsible for can be designated to be available to answer questions and assist the new teachers for a period (say, at least two weeks). It is better if the role of the buddy is specified in a clear way so that both parties know what to expect. In some cases, the buddy is offered extra pay or is released from some teaching to enable them to carry out their buddy duties. In some cases, the supportive relationship between the buddy and new teacher may continue for a longer period and develop into mentoring (see Chapter 5).

Activity 2.6 Write short guidelines for a buddy to work with the new teacher recruited to Institution A (in Activity 2.1), bearing in mind that the buddy will have only one hour a week for two weeks to do this extra work.

Conclusion

This chapter has offered simple but detailed guidance for LCMs on teacher recruitment. There are many potential alternative procedures, and those adopted are likely to depend on national legislation and customs, as well as on institutional policy, the urgency of the situation, and the ease or difficulty of attracting suitable candidates. The LCM's objectives are, of course, to appoint the best possible teachers for the job and the institutional culture, and to ensure that the new members of staff fully understand the requirements and terms and conditions of the post, and the challenges and opportunities their work will entail. Clarity, transparency, and a welcoming approach are all essential, and the efficiency and quality of the procedures used during recruitment and induction will be indications of the quality standards expected by the institution.

PART TWO

3 WORKING WITH TEACHERS: MANAGEMENT, SUPPORT, AND COMMUNICATION

Introduction

This chapter discusses some of the challenges faced by LCMs in building, maintaining, and managing teams of teachers. In many institutions teachers are very well managed and appreciate the way they are managed, which implies that in most situations LCMs deal with the challenges well, although it is surprising how quickly things can sometimes change.

When things are going well:

- The LCM is **authoritative** rather than **authoritarian**, demands much from the teaching team and yet is responsive, and is firm but not rigidly so.
- There are good relations between all members of staff, a sense that they are all contributing to the common good and to the successful fulfilment of the institution's purpose.
- There is quite a lot of innovation and creativity on all sides. People are happy to float ideas, and don't get upset if they don't lead anywhere, but often they feed discussion and do lead to a new development.
- People are business-like and take their work seriously, but in between there is a lot of sharing at a personal level, as well as about work-related issues.
- There is also time for fun and relaxation when there is an occasion to be marked.
- Even if they do not have a lot of time, people like the challenge of new projects and the opportunity to bounce ideas and experiences off one another.
- New members of the team immediately feel welcome and are helped to settle in quickly. If anyone has a difficulty of a professional or personal nature, including the LCM, there is a general sense of concern and a willingness to help.

This may sound idyllic and, of course, it may not be the reality all the time, especially when employment conditions are precarious or there is a downturn in the institution's fortunes or external pressure on it. But such a scenario is far from unusual, partly because we all like to feel productive and comfortable at work, and many LCMs and teachers, if not a majority, have experienced such a work environment at some point in their careers.

The management of the team

The job of a teacher in an institution often involves working alone with students for a majority of the time. This can make the work rather lonely or quite exhilarating, depending on the individual, the context or class, or even the day of the week. The loneliness can be especially difficult when teachers are out of their depth because of the type of course, unexpected issues that arise within the class, such as low motivation, disruption, or conflict between students, and where the situation does not improve from lesson to lesson with that group. It is thus important that teachers, not just newly appointed staff, feel able to turn to others for support, both to a manager and to colleagues.

Even confident and successful teachers should not be left to their own devices. They should be encouraged to interact with their manager and other colleagues at more than just a social level. The team needs them, especially as they may be able to support less confident and less experienced colleagues, and, indeed, the manager. Certain teachers may sometimes see themselves as free to do professionally as they see fit in their day-to-day work without reference to anyone else, but as employees they represent the organization and, when they agreed to be employed, they also agreed to work collaboratively towards its mission and objectives.

From the institution's point of view, it is important that teachers and all staff work as a team. This is not because they need to spend a lot of time working on tasks together, although there are times when it is necessary to do so. On the contrary, in some settings, teachers see little of each other because they are teaching off-site or at times of the day when other colleagues are not working. These teachers too are part of the wider organization, however, and are representing it, and interpreting the curriculum and following the guidelines provided. From a professional point of view, teachers need to feel that they can contribute to the organization's development in some way, that they can share in the exchange of expertise, and can seek support from, and offer support to, their colleagues.

There are many kinds of teams in education. It is worth spending a moment considering what the characteristics of good teams should be.

Activity 3.1 — Think of the institutions where you have worked as a manager or teacher. Given that experience, what do you consider to be the three most important characteristics or features of a well-functioning team in a language institution, both from the academic manager's point of view and from that of the teachers?

Figure 3.1 lists some of the main characteristics of an effective team, contrasted with features that indicate an ineffective team.

In effective teams, people:	In ineffective teams, people:
• are clear about the aims of the institution and team • have clearly defined roles • have opportunities for participation in collective work • have good personal relations • have a commitment to and pride in the work • share ideas and opinions • have shared ownership of challenges • participate in decisions	• have no sense of purpose • do not have clearly defined roles • have impersonal relationships and work in isolation • have little chance to share expertise and contribute to decisions • have little personal commitment to the work or to collaboration with colleagues • have little will to improve or develop • have low morale and a sense of alienation from the employer

Figure 3.1 Characteristics of effective and ineffective teams (adapted from Eaquals, 2004)

Activity 3.2 Compare Figure 3.1 with your own list from Activity 3.1, adding any features you consider to be missing in the left-hand column. Which of these features, if any, are not present in the teaching team in the institution where you work?

It is essential that managers establish ways and means and the right conditions to ensure that teachers work collaboratively with one another for the common good and follow institutional policies and procedures. This need not mean that quieter individuals in the team should be constantly pressured to participate in team activities, or that the teachers' room is always a noisy social space. It is a case of finding the right balance between focused individual preparation and delivery of teaching on the one hand, and collegial professional engagement on the other.

Activity 3.3 As an LCM, what three key steps would you take (or have you taken) to ensure that teachers do not only work in isolation and do engage in collegial interaction as members of a team?

There are no easy answers but there are three general common-sense guidelines to be followed. First, it is essential that LCMs make clear how they prefer and expect to work with the teaching team, especially how they intend to communicate with them, and the kind of atmosphere they want to encourage. LCMs usually have a number of administrative duties that require concentration and quiet, but being available for the teaching team means ensuring that the door is almost always open, and that the LCM is together with the teachers at certain times, such as first thing in the day when things can go wrong—for example, because of sudden absence or lateness or unexpected visits—as well as at break times and at the end of the teachers' working day. Even this may not be easy: teachers may be spread over several sites, or work different hours, in which case, efforts have to be made to at least rotate to the different teaching locations and to be available at different times on different days.

Second, when meeting with teachers in this way, it helps if LCMs do more than make general conversation; talking about specific details to do with students or classes is a good way to engage with individual teachers and support them in their work. Putting teachers with common challenges in touch with each other, or talking about individual teachers' lives outside the institution, are other possible ways in which the LCM can develop and maintain an open ongoing relationship between LCMs and teachers. Being a good listener is key, as is demonstrating a genuine interest in teachers' work and concerns. However, LCMs also need to be open about the challenges and limitations they are dealing with as LCMs without complaining excessively, and about their expectations of teachers.

Third, it is important for LCMs to be clear in their own mind, and then to indicate to teachers, which decisions the team can be involved in. The extent to which decisions can be shared about the structure of the timetable, the courses to be delivered, the teaching and learning materials which can be used, and who teaches which class varies from institution to institution. Even in institutions where opportunities for involving teachers in such decisions are limited, the LCM can ask teachers beforehand to express and explain their preferences as regards the courses they would ideally like to teach. But teachers need to understand that the LCM represents the employer and thus needs to implement policy and ensure that teachers do what they are required to and that the right decisions are made from the institution's and the students' point of view, which may sometimes involve disagreement. There are no easy ways around this delicate balance but the suggestions in Figure 3.2 may help LCMs to avoid uncomfortable situations. A common thread in Figure 3.2 is that LCMs need to make the reasons for their decisions clear from the beginning and, if necessary, to repeat these reasons later on. Doing so helps avoid false expectations, and helps LCMs communicate a sense of fairness and consistency in the way they manage teachers.

People management: some challenges

So far in this chapter, we have dealt mainly with the LCM's role in and approach to managing the teaching team from an administrative perspective. The management of individual teachers and subgroups of them probably takes up more of the LCM's time, and it brings into focus the less-easy-to-manage issues that may crop up in diverse teams. In a language teaching institution, these problematic aspects of people management may include the following challenges:

- teachers who apparently do not wish to be, and do not behave as, members of the team – the loners
- teachers who are unhappy about or feel alienated from the institution as their employer, but don't intend to leave – the disaffected
- teachers who do things their own way, whatever procedures and rules may exist – let's call them the mavericks.

This is not, of course, to suggest that all teachers fall into one of these loose categories: in most institutions, there would be at most one or two in any of them.

WHAT	HOW
Be open about the constraints of the LCM's role. In particular, the need to ensure that the best possible service is provided to all students.	Make this clear at the beginning of each course period, as well as during the induction of new teachers. Statements such as the following may help: 'It won't be possible to give all teachers the timetables and classes they would prefer, but timetabling will be done as fairly as possible, taking into account your experience and your preferences.'
Avoid the temptation to give in to insistent teachers' requests. Teachers, like students, are sensitive to any signs of favouritism.	This can be difficult when teachers offer what seem to be genuine reasons why they need to avoid certain times or types of classes, but so long as there is fair rotation of less convenient timetables and less popular classes from one teaching period to the next, impartiality can be maintained and be seen to be maintained.
Avoid allowing teachers to teach mainly the classes they are comfortable with because they have done so before, or because they want to avoid the challenge of teaching a new level or age group.	As part of the induction, and regularly with current teachers, it needs to be made clear that part of the LCM's job is to steadily increase the versatility of teachers through new challenges, supported by mentoring and CPD, and to point out the potential development benefits of this to teachers.
Ensure that basic standards of punctuality and administrative work related to student attendance, records of work covered, attendance at obligatory group meetings, etc. are maintained.	Explain regularly why punctuality, record keeping, and participation in administrative meetings are important, speaking to teachers individually about any omissions on their part. When the problem persists, have an individual meeting to explore the reasons why and reinforce the policy.

Figure 3.2 Suggestions for establishing good working relations with teachers

In the section below, some of the challenges posed by teachers with these characteristics are discussed in further detail, and suggestions are made as to how LCMs can deal with them. But it has to be remembered that each teacher is an individual with their own unique character, background, and qualities, so it is wise to reflect very carefully before deciding how to respond in each individual case.

The loners

Some teachers are less team-orientated than others. There may be various reasons for this, such as:
- a desire to do things in one's own way
- a reluctance or shyness about sharing ideas and materials
- a lack of confidence
- a desire for privacy and independence
- a fear of change and innovation
- a desire to restrict the workload.

Being a loner is not necessarily a bad thing for teachers—some people are naturally less sociable and more private than others—but it can pose small problems for LCMs, who may be concerned about whether all is well with such teachers, whether they need help, and also whether their general quietness is a sign of discontent. Certainly, such individuals should not be left out of the discussions just because they are quiet. It may also be useful to encourage them to work with someone else on a project such as peer observation or materials development. Forcing them to participate in team work, however, is unlikely to succeed. They need to take their own time.

The disaffected

Some experienced or very self-sufficient teachers may, for various reasons, display a more negative attitude, which can be unsettling for LCMs to deal with and can have an effect on the whole team, especially if teachers who share the same attitudes band together in a subgroup.

Activity 3.4   Look at the list of statements below. What kind of thinking is behind them? How can an LCM try to counteract this kind of thinking?

We've always done it like this. Why change? What's wrong with the current system?
It won't work.
I told you it wouldn't work.
It's not my problem.
It's management's fault.
They're taking advantage of me.
It's not my job, it's not what I'm paid for.

(Adapted from Eaquals, 2004)

There are various things that LCMs can try in order to counteract such sentiments. These include:

- recognizing that there is a problem and asking the teacher(s) concerned to express their views frankly to the LCM so that there can be a discussion: this can bring genuinely felt problems out into the open and possibly begin the process of resolving them
- showing that the LCM and the institution cares about each individual teacher: often negative or uncooperative attitudes stem from a sense that the institution does not treat its teachers in a caring way and does not respect their professionalism or their views; this can be compounded by employment conditions that are 'precarious' or unfavourable in other ways
- adopting the approach, especially at times when there is high pressure, that 'we're all in this together', and reminding individuals that the LCM is also under pressure
- getting the team, especially any disruptive subgroup, to help solve problems and to identify changes that may be helpful, and consulting with them about options
- ensuring that concerns about employment or contract issues, and other misunderstandings, are dealt with quickly and sensitively.

Such approaches can do a lot to encourage greater ownership and promote a more positive atmosphere. However, in some cases, there may be a need for the LCM to try to reduce resistance and develop a greater sense of collective responsibility over the long term. For example, it is important for everyone to be open and direct during group and individual meetings. Encouraging team members to express their concerns openly, even if not in public, for example by asking them individually whether they have a worry about a specific decision or course of action, can also help to create this climate of openness. Finally, it is important to ensure that the handling of complaints or dissatisfaction is methodical and fair, that the procedures are known to everyone, and in particular, that genuine concerns are not dealt with lightly or brushed off, even if they seem to the LCM to be unjustified.

The mavericks

There is something quite attractive about people who seem to have little respect for the general written or unwritten rules. Students seem to appreciate teachers who dress in an exotic way, possibly breaching the institution's dress code, and those who have unusual mannerisms or ways of dealing with students. From the LCM's point of view, however, teachers who persistently arrive late or miss parts of meetings, do not record and hand in test results, or ignore guidelines about student homework can be problematic. Apart from the quality issues mentioned above, the question of equal rights and opportunities arises. If it is institutional policy that all students should have a homework task once a week, but two or three teachers never set homework, this could be seen as putting their students at a disadvantage (even if the students are happy not to have homework). In addition, there is the question of equality between staff members: arguably, by not doing paperwork relating to student attendance and assessments and not assigning or marking homework, some teachers are having an easier life by avoiding certain responsibilities in their job description. Other teachers might feel either aggrieved or that they should follow the example of the maverick. However hard it can be to ensure that everyone is following the set procedures and doing their job as intended, it is essential that LCMs do not ignore the mavericks and instead find ways to impose at least a degree of compliance.

Managing serious disagreements and disciplinary problems

In certain circumstances, there may be a confrontation between the LCM and one or more teachers of the types identified above, especially the disaffected but potentially the mavericks as well. For the sake of harmony and the general well-being of the team, such confrontations are to be avoided or kept private if possible, but it is equally harmful to allow open hostility or discourteous and uncooperative behaviour to go unchallenged. For example, a situation where rules and procedures, such as those to do with attending staff meetings or submitting student records, are followed by the majority but flouted by a few cannot be allowed to continue. Similarly, if the LCM makes a principled decision but certain teachers refuse to go along with it, the situation cannot be ignored in the hope that they will change their minds later. Managing such confrontations requires resilience, preparation and skill. Let us consider two such potential situations:

Situation A is in a group meeting. During the meeting, a teacher loses their temper with the LCM and starts loudly protesting about a given decision or situation. This teacher is then supported by one or two others, who share the same views.

Situation B is in a school. The LCM is aware that a teacher, who generally falls into the disaffected category due to historical and personal reasons, is covertly stirring up resistance and hostility towards decisions without actually expressing disagreement in a clear and rational way.

Neither of these situations can be allowed to pass. In Situation A, the LCM would be wise to remain calm and not to engage in a bitter argument with the teachers concerned during the meeting. The option of simply adjourning the meeting can be a good way of showing that the behaviour is not acceptable and is regarded as seriously disruptive. But in addition, the LCM needs to immediately organize a meeting with the individual or subgroup concerned. Whether this is to be seen as a disciplinary meeting will depend on the circumstances, but in most contexts open hostility between members of staff and refusal to accept management decisions are seen as disciplinary matters. In Situation B, things are less clear since the disciplinary aspect depends on the evidence that someone is deliberately stirring up discontent and dissent. Nevertheless, it is necessary to bring the matter out into the open, starting with a meeting with the individual or individuals involved.

In both cases, the teachers in question may have a reasonable point to make, at least from their own points of view, but given that there is potentially a disciplinary aspect to the proposed meetings, it is very important for the LCM to be properly prepared and to plan the steps of the meeting. In particular, the LCM needs to be very familiar with the institution's disciplinary and grievance procedures: what course of action should be followed by managers when a member of staff behaves in an unacceptable way and how should complaints about the institution and its managers be handled? The LCM would be wise to get advice from the person in charge of human resources if there is any uncertainty. It would be unfortunate, for example, if a meeting which was intended to improve the situation actually made matters worse. A possible course of action is described as follows: the explanation for the meeting should be given at the beginning, and may involve explaining why the behaviour is or was unacceptable from the LCM's point of view. Then teachers need to be offered an opportunity to explain and apologize for their behaviour. They may not do so or, in the case of Situation B mentioned above, they may deny that their behaviour is unacceptable. Here, it is important that the discussion of the point of disagreement and the issue of unacceptable behaviour are kept separate. The LCM needs to carefully consider and respond to the point of disagreement, whether or not any resolution or compromise can be reached, while ensuring that the issue of unacceptable behaviour is firmly spelled out. In relation to disagreement, the LCM can remind the teacher(s), how grievances and complaints from staff are dealt with, so that there is clarity about that. Of course, any warnings given to teachers will depend on the institution's policy which, in turn, may depend on national legislation or specific employment agreements but may, for example, involve at least an escalation from a verbal to a written warning. Again, teachers should have this information in their contracts but disciplinary policy can be restated. Finally, a decision needs to be taken about whether or not a written record is kept, whether teachers will see the record, and who else will read it.

The overall aim is, of course, that the meeting will end reasonably amicably with the teachers concerned feeling that they have been fairly treated, but now have a better understanding of what is expected of them and how they should in future deal with their disagreements and concerns. It is essential that the LCM's comments should be very clear and that they remain as unemotional as possible while being firm and matter-of-fact. While representing the institution as an employer, the LCM needs to maintain as positive as possible a working relation with all teachers. Of course, in certain cases, the relationship may break down irrevocably and dismissal or non-renewal of a contract may be the eventual last resort, depending on the seriousness of the case and relevant legislation.

Activity 3.5

Consider situations A–C. Decide what the 'real' reasons for the behaviour and/or point of view are, and list what action could be taken and/or what procedure could be adopted to put things right.

Situation A: Three teachers complain that there is little opportunity for exchange of ideas and lesson plans in the current set-up. Teachers are left largely to their own devices, and any meetings that take place usually focus on administration. The teachers are worried that standards are suffering because of a lack of consistency of content between different teachers' classes.

Situation B: Two students from the same class have complained about their two teachers. The LCM needs to review the folder containing attendance and lesson records, but it is not where it should be. When it is finally found, the LCM discovers that the lesson record sheets, which should be completed for every lesson, are not filled in, and so she cannot find out what has been going on in the course.

Situation C: A teacher more than once makes it clear that he does not believe in using the systems and procedures set up to ensure consistency and high quality in teaching and course administration. His attitude is: 'I give good, entertaining lessons, the students are happy with what I provide. Why should I conform to time-consuming procedures which I don't think work?'

(Adapted from Eaquals, 2004)

Such situations potentially affect not only the cohesiveness and smooth functioning of the institution but also the quality of the services provided to the main customers, i.e. the students. Situations B and C in particular illustrate the tension between individuals and the team, especially when, through an unwillingness to conform, individuals refuse to follow procedures or implement decisions. In such cases, it is important to remind teachers why the procedures exist or why the decision was made, and to point out that their lack of cooperation affects the institution and overall quality. In the case of procedures, it may be worth periodically reviewing these from time to time, especially those procedures which are not being properly applied. The LCM can organize a meeting with the whole team for that purpose. In this process, the key question for the group to discuss, or perhaps smaller subgroups if there are several policies to be looked at, are:

- Why do we have this procedure or rule? What is its purpose?
- Do you agree that it's still necessary? If not, why?
- Why do you think it isn't being used properly by some members of staff?
- Are there ways in which we can improve or streamline the procedure?

Clearly, in any such discussion it is important that the LCM does not give the impression that existing procedures and rules or earlier decisions can be abolished or overturned by democratic consensus – unless the management team also believe they are no longer necessary. The aim of the discussion is to get the team to 'buy into' the systems in place and to get everybody using them consistently, by inviting the team to participate in improving processes for the benefit of all, where possible.

In the case of Situation A, there is a golden opportunity for the LCM and teachers to discuss whether a new way of working should be established. In such cases, it is best if the teachers proposing a different way of doing things are willing to be public advocates, so that the team can see how initiatives to innovate and improve don't come only from the LCM.

It is of course possible that these measures will not work with people who, for whatever reason, have decided not to be cooperative. Assuming that they are doing their teaching job properly, there is no point in the LCM worrying unduly about it. But there is no need to give up entirely. An opportunity may present itself to attract the individual(s) in question to work on certain projects that interest them or to take responsibility for mentoring less experienced teachers.

Meetings and other communications

Relations between LCMs and teachers involve both informal individual encounters, and more organized and formal events, such as meetings, which have the function of ensuring that the team all receive and can respond to the same information and instructions at the same time, as well as written emails and notices (discussed in more detail in the next section). Ways of planning, running, and following up these meetings are discussed below.

Causes of dissatisfaction with meetings

An area that LCMs often find difficult and that causes dissatisfaction among teachers is the handling of meetings and other communications about practical and administrative matters. The focus here is not on workshops for INSET or CPD, which are considered in detail in Chapter 4, but the routine contacts that are necessary for the smooth running of courses.

Activity 3.6

In your experience as an LCM or a teacher, consider which four of the following are most likely to cause a sense of dissatisfaction in face-to-face group meetings:

1. A lack of clear objectives and/or agenda for the meeting
2. The length of the meeting
3. The timing of the meeting in the working day
4. The frequency of meetings
5. Unconstructive discussion
6. Long explanations from the manager and/or long interventions from teachers
7. Unwillingness of some teachers to participate
8. Too little consultation about important matters
9. Too much consultation about trivial matters
10. A lack of clear decisions at the end of the meeting

Practical concerns

Without going through all the possible things that can go wrong at meetings (such as people arriving late or the room where it is held being unsuitable), simple questions for the LCM to think about when organizing the meeting can help avoid difficulties:

- Is this one of the regular meetings held, for example, every week?
- What are the objectives for this meeting? Is the meeting mainly to pass on information, or is it partly to consult or seek consensus on a decision (e.g. about a procedure, materials or tests, the curriculum, students, and so on)?
- Is it obligatory for all teachers (i.e. part of their contract), or voluntary for some? Does everyone need to be present, or does it concern a subgroup of teachers only?
- Are teachers allowed to add points of their own to the agenda?
- How long will the meeting take?
- Who will run it? How will it be run?
- What record will be made of the points addressed? How will this be communicated to those concerned?
- Considering the above, is this particular meeting necessary? Why/Why not?

It is worth asking oneself such questions even if the meeting is routine and obligatory, and using the answers to prepare for the meeting. It might even be possible to cancel or postpone the meeting if, after answering the above questions, it seems unnecessary.

Logistical problems organizing teachers' meetings

Several institutions find it difficult to hold group meetings with teachers for various reasons. For example, there may be too large a number of teachers (one Eaquals school has over 150), and/or the teachers may have very different timetables so are not available at the same time.

It may be preferable or necessary for the LCM to hold smaller meetings for groups of teachers, for example those teaching at primary level separately from those teaching at secondary level, and of course, those teaching at one location separately from those at others. However, not all items require a meeting: the 'for information' items could be communicated in another way, and even consultation can take place remotely. Email is one alternative means, and a private Facebook page or school intranet are others. Videoconference applications, such as Skype and Adobe Connect (see Website references), enable groups of up to 25 to communicate, and are certainly convenient for small groups since they offer the possibility of sharing computer screens, as well as using written instant messages synchronously with the video discussion. This does not mean that the handling of communications is any easier – they may be just as challenging. In general terms, the same guidelines apply whether addressing a group of teachers face to face or remotely, and whether using the spoken or written word.

Meeting agendas

Preparing a simple agenda for a meeting, especially a routine administrative one, will often test how necessary the meeting is and indicate how it needs to be run. The agenda should include the start time, end time, and location, as well as indicate in order of importance what will be raised or discussed. Where the focus of the meeting is giving information, items can be under a heading indicating this (see Figure 3.3), while items that need to be decided can appear in a separate list. It is a good idea to make the agenda available to teachers a day or two before the meeting by posting it in the staffroom and/or emailing it to them. Time at the meeting can also be saved if teachers are sent relevant documents to read beforehand, or tasks or questionnaires to complete.

Teachers' meeting: Friday 10th, 13.15-13.45 (room 6)

For information:
- Courses starting next Monday – see attached list
- Assessments for this week: what and when
- Room 15 refurbishment
- Extracurricular events
- Notes and action points from the last meeting

For discussion and decision:
- Changes to the B2 syllabus – see attached revision
- Next week's CPD workshop
- Other points (add items below, together with your initials, or email me)

Note: please read the attached documents ahead of the meeting.

Figure 3.3 Sample staff meeting agenda

Managing meetings

Activity 3.7

A colleague who is new to managing teachers has asked you for advice about running a teachers' meeting and communicating with teachers by email.

What are the three most important suggestions you would make about handling each situation?

The advice will depend in part on the context, the number and the characteristics of the teachers involved, and the type of issues that are dealt with at meetings. Some suggested advice for this LCM is offered in Figure 3.4.

Do	Don't
- prepare properly and arrive on time
- encourage teachers to adopt the habit of reading relevant documents beforehand, pointing out that this will save meeting time and prepare them better for discussion
- consider displaying the agenda and other relevant documents on a projector, especially if the meeting is crowded
- call the meeting to order and confirm the agenda, asking if anything else needs adding, or if anything needs to be clarified
- establish rules for asking questions and intervening if necessary, such as raising a hand
- go through action points from the previous meeting, expressing satisfaction and/or congratulations for certain completed items, and dwelling on action points that still need attention
- speak clearly and refer to relevant documents, then ask if there are any questions
- make it very clear, before starting the 'for discussion' items, what points the team can have an influence on and what is not negotiable, as well as whether the purpose is to reach a consensus or just to gather opinions so that you can decide later
- get the teachers who added a proposal to the agenda to introduce their points in favour of it
- summarize any points made by various people when discussion time is up, as well as what the decision is or when the decision will be made
- finish the meeting on time with a brief summary, telling people when written minutes will be circulated and/or displayed
- prepare and share brief meeting minutes on each item, with action points, the initials of those responsible, and deadlines, where necessary
- refer to these meeting minutes at the next meeting, making sure the action points are dealt with, or that people are informed of the reasons why not	- improvise or be too casual
- expect people to remember what the items on the agenda are
- allow people to chat or distract each other while the meeting is in progress
- mumble or rush through items, or assume that people will have read the documents or notices beforehand
- read aloud from documents without explaining what you are reading
- forget to refer back to the previous meeting and review the action points that were listed in the minutes
- rush to the next point before people have had a chance to ask questions
- allow arguments to start before discussion items have been properly introduced and the choices clearly outlined
- immediately contradict people who make suggestions that you don't agree with
- let one person dominate the discussion so that others don't get a chance to express themselves
- let the discussion get out of hand so that it is hard to follow what is going on
- move on until everyone is clear about what the decision is or when it will be made
- run over time unless there is general consent to this
- end the meeting without making clear what has been decided and when minutes will be circulated/displayed
- forget to write up notes or organize for the action points to be dealt with
- forget at the next meeting to mention what actions have been completed and, if any have not, the reasons for this

Figure 3.4 'Dos and don'ts' for managing teachers' meetings

After the meeting

Where meetings of any kind are concerned, an important consideration is what happens afterwards. The discipline of meeting notes or minutes, however short, with clear action points indicating who will do what by when is a useful one, as it provides reminders and connections between successive meetings, especially when there are gaps. This is only effective, however, if the LCM takes time at a relevant point in the next meeting to go through the action points, reminding people which points have been successfully dealt with, and how (this may be an opportunity to thank or congratulate an individual or group on their work). This is also a good opportunity for the LCM to focus on pending action points by asking for progress reports, discussing any difficulties that have arisen, and perhaps extending the deadline. This is especially important if the action point was to be dealt with by the LCM: they will need to explain in a matter-of-fact way why it was not possible and what will now happen. Honesty is the best policy, but setting oneself realistic deadlines and meeting them is better still. Everyone, including the LCM, will take a more positive view of meetings if they see that they lead somewhere, that they are an effective mechanism for decision-making and development, as well as for sharing information and ideas.

Other reasons for meetings

Apart from the obvious need to regularly discuss matters related to delivering courses and running the institution, there are other good reasons to hold meetings that may not be mentioned in an agenda. One of them concerns the team: bringing the team together in one place can remind teachers that they are not just working as individuals. Another related reason may be to introduce someone new to the group: newly appointed teachers or other staff members, or even certain visitors, will much more readily feel welcome if they have been included in routine group events. And then there are dynamic or social reasons: where teachers are starting the working day at the same time, for example, some LCMs like to bring them together for a few minutes to greet them and inform them about something relevant for that day – new students, new resources, an examination, a birthday, and so on.

Written communications with teachers

Where face-to-face meetings are supplemented by written communication, especially where meetings are not possible for a longer period and are replaced by emails, it is important to bear in mind the certain key points that may increase or reduce the effectiveness of them. As is well known, a danger with emails or social networking posts is that the sheer quantity that any individual has to read is in itself a problem. Making the subject very clear in the heading and indicating its urgency through a deadline can help the LCM to highlight important emails. Keeping the communication as short as possible while making the key points very clear, for example using bullets, numbers, and underlining, and putting them in a sequential order can also help. Such communications do not need to be formal, but a neutral tone is better than 'jokey' informality, especially in emails going to a large group of people. Where the communication is addressed to an individual, it is best to use their name, and mail merge features can be easily enabled so that even group emails can be addressed to each person by name. Finally, by encouraging people to get in touch by phone or face to face if they need clarification or wish to discuss something is a good way for the LCM to counteract the remote nature of such communications.

A two-way process

Meetings and other forms of communication with teachers are important and unavoidable ways of 'oiling the wheels' of language course management, and the ways in which the LCM handles these communications can make a big difference to the prevailing climate in the staffroom. But, of course, the process of gaining the confidence and achieving an open and productive relationship with teachers involves much more than good communication.

Activity 3.8 What steps can be taken by LCMs to encourage teachers to be more open to self-assessment, reflection, and dialogue about their work?

There are several steps that can be taken to promote a more open climate between managers and teachers, as well as other staff members. Blumberg and Jonas (1987) conducted research in which they asked teachers (not specifically language teachers) about 'highly productive relationships' with supervisors (for further discussion on this research, see *Language Teacher Supervision* by Bailey, 2006, p. 284). They found 12 teachers who were able to describe the behaviours of supervisors that had helped to make the relationships productive. These behaviours included:

- a collaborative approach to problem-solving
- making teachers feel they are experts on teaching
- making teachers feel they are intelligent
- making teachers feel they are being listened to
- as supervisors, being open about what they do and do not know
- being interested in teachers as people.

(Blumberg & Jonas, 1987, pp. 60–61)

There are some clear lessons to be learned or confirmed from research like this. To establish the kind of relationship that is needed in order to make discussion around teacher development needs and plans productive from both parties' points of view, the LCM needs to work on building up teachers' confidence—including their confidence in the manager—promoting and engaging in a team approach, and following the same guidelines as other members of staff. When confidence-building, staff members need to feel 'safe' in the sense that LCMs care about them as people, that they can communicate freely with them, and that engaging with procedures and activities set up by the institution will be beneficial, not disadvantageous, in some way. In order to gain this kind of confidence, teachers need to:

- understand and consent to the procedures or initiatives being used or proposed – for example, to identify possible development needs: this requires LCMs to clearly explain the procedures and their benefits, and give teachers opportunities to discuss them and perhaps suggest changes
- feel that they are being dealt with and will continue to be dealt with as individuals, and that any specific needs and preferences they have will be taken into account – for example, some members of staff are shyer than others, or less comfortable with sudden changes of plan, while others are more laid back and less prone to stress
- feel good about important aspects of their work, not just through regular praise (which may sound artificial or even patronising) but through a sense that they are gaining and showing expertise on however small a scale, and that this is recognized – for example, good work with intermediate level students might result in the LCM asking a teacher to help a less experienced teacher working with intermediate students for the first time.

Conclusion

This chapter has considered the importance of creating and maintaining a willingness and, where possible, an enthusiasm among teachers to work as a team and to bear in mind the needs of the institution and colleagues, as well as their own individual preferences and priorities. On the one hand, teachers need to feel that their professionalism and competence is acknowledged and respected, but on the other hand, they need to be aware that the organization and management of courses requires principled decision-making, clear procedures, and often compromises, all of which involves maintaining a productive ongoing relationship and regular communication. This implies that meetings with teachers and other forms of communication with them need careful preparation and skilful handling by the LCM. At the same time, teachers need to feel that they are able to contribute ideas that may improve things, not just from their own individual perspective but for the team as a whole. In other words, the climate and ethos fostered by the LCM should be such that each person and the whole team sees it as their responsibility not just to deliver effective teaching but to participate in the overall development of quality in the institution. This includes individual and collective professional development, which are the topics of the next three chapters.

4 ASSESSING TEACHERS' DEVELOPMENT NEEDS

Introduction

Chapters 2 and 3 have explored the practical aspects of recruiting, inducting and orientating, and managing the day-to-day work of teachers – the 'nuts and bolts' of human resources management where teachers are concerned. The differences between teachers as individuals and the teaching team were also discussed. In this chapter, the focus is on another important area of staff management: assessing and identifying their professional development needs. While the focus here is on teacher development, it is important not to forget that all staff members, including LCMs themselves, have professional development needs that should be acknowledged and, in relevant cases, supported by the institution.

The first book in this series, *Language Teaching Competences*, explores teacher professional development from various angles and provides examples of tools that can be used for teacher self-assessment and/or joint assessment as a means of stimulating reflection about individual development needs and wants. In this chapter we will focus on identifying and agreeing teacher development priorities, and the ways in which the LCM can achieve a balance between the needs of individual teachers, those of the teaching team, and the institution's own requirements.

Balancing teacher development priorities

As was pointed out in *Language Teaching Competences*, teacher development can be defined as 'a bottom-up process and as such can be contrasted with top-down staff development programmes ... [and] is independent of the organization but often functioning more successfully with its support and recognition' (Mann, 2005, p. 105). It is therefore important to ensure that the support and recognition of the institution really does contribute to genuine teacher development at an individual level, and that the whole teaching team feel supported in their development as a group. This does not mean that the institution should simply respond to requests for support from individuals and the team rather than providing support that the employers consider important, which will mainly focus on ensuring that its students are effectively helped with their learning. Rather, the art of providing such support hinges on the LCM's ability to be in tune with the development needs of teachers while also being able to ensure that the institution's requirements for quality and effectiveness in language education are being met. Figure 4.1 shows how these interrelate.

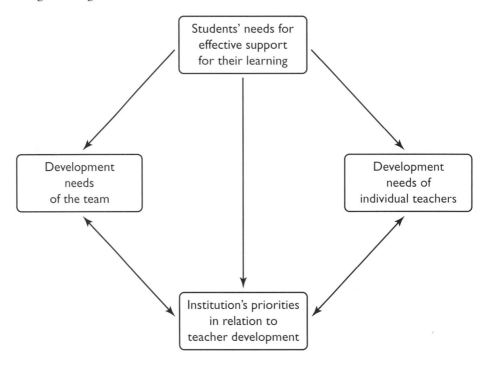

Figure 4.1 Needs to be considered when planning support for teacher development

Activity 4.1 In your experience of working in language education, which development needs were given priority: those of individual teachers, those of the whole teaching team, or the needs of the institution itself?

In most cases, achieving a balance between these overlapping needs is quite hard, partly because the respective needs may not be articulated clearly, or because it may be difficult to achieve consensus, first on what the development needs are from each point of view, and second on which are more important and deserve more attention. Much depends on the context of the teaching institution and the nature of the teaching team. It could be argued that, ideally, if teacher development is the responsibility mainly of individual teachers, it is they who should do most of the deciding about priorities. But here we are mainly concerned with teachers working for an institution, not freelance teachers working independently with students they have signed up themselves, so articulating, harmonizing, and balancing the needs of individuals with those of the team and those of the institution has to be a key aim of any LCM. Needless to say, these development needs are subject to the budget constraints of the institution.

Assessing teachers' development needs

In many contexts it may anyway be quite hard for teachers to identify their development needs and priorities without help. As Maingay (1988) pointed out, 'much of what a teacher does in a language teaching classroom is ritual behaviour rather than principled behaviour' (p. 119), and getting back to principles from rituals can be easier if key questions are discussed with the LCM as a means of raising awareness and getting teachers to think (again) about what they do, and draw their attention to 'the principles behind the rituals' (p. 119). The next section examines psychological aspects of the relationship between LCMs and teachers in some detail, and seeks to describe some of the complexity of that relationship from the perspective of counselling.

The scope of intervention with teachers

Writers such as Randall & Thornton (2001) and Kurtoglu-Hooten (2016) have seen Heron's work on intervention analysis as useful in supporting and supervising teachers. In this model, derived from the field of psychological and emotional counselling, Heron (2001) posited six potential categories of intervention that counselling practitioners might use with their 'clients'. These are shown in Figure 4.2.

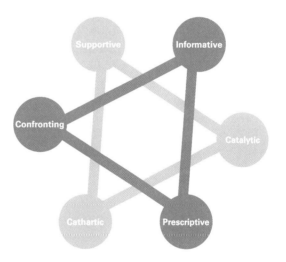

Figure 4.2 Six categories of intervention (Heron, 2001)

As can be seen, the six categories are arranged in two overlapping triangles. In one triangle, the interventions are described as 'authoritative'; these interventions are 'prescriptive', 'informative', and 'confronting'. The following is a summary of the aims of these types of intervention:

Prescriptive: 'to direct the behaviour of the client, usually behaviour that is outside the practitioner-client relationship'

Informative: 'to impart knowledge, information, meaning to the client'

Confronting: 'to raise the client's consciousness about some limiting attitude or behaviour of which they are relatively unaware'

(Adapted from Heron, 2001, pp. 5–6)

In the other triangle, the interventions are 'facilitative', i.e. designed to help the client in some way. These are labelled 'supportive', 'catalytic', and 'cathartic'. Heron summarizes the aims of these interventions as follows:

> Cathartic: 'to enable the client to … abreact painful emotion, primarily grief, fear and anger'
>
> Catalytic: 'to elicit self-discovery, self-directed living, learning and problem-solving'
>
> Supportive: 'to affirm the worth and value of the client's person, qualities, attitudes and actions'

(Adapted from Heron, 2001, p. 6)

There are questions to be asked about whether parallels can or should be drawn between LCMs and the teachers they work with on the one hand, and counsellors and their clients on the other. There is undoubtedly a need for LCMs to offer both direction and support to teachers, but the nature of the relationship is not the same as the very sensitive relationship between a counsellor and a client who has approached or been referred to the counsellor for help that is in many cases expected to be life-changing. Nevertheless, distinguishing and balancing the two main types of intervention is helpful because it is a reminder of the dual nature of the teacher–LCM relationship. Facilitative interactions, in which teachers are given opportunities to let off steam—in Heron's terms, to 'abreact painful emotion'—need to be skilfully combined with interactions which seek to direct teachers' behaviour, to share knowledge and information, and to raise teachers' awareness about attitudes or behaviours that are 'limiting'.

Activity 4.2   Do you find Heron's distinction between 'authoritative' and 'facilitative' interactions relevant to the management and support of teachers? Think of instances from your own experience that have involved either or both kinds of interaction between an LCM and a teacher. What effect did the interactions have? How productive were they, and in what ways?

How do such ideas fit in with teacher development? First and foremost, they are a reminder that both teachers and LCMs are people with their own personalities, emotions, preferences, and challenges. Unlike many of the clients that counsellors deal with, teachers are exposed on a daily basis to the particular strains of dealing with groups of students who are, in many senses, the teachers' own 'clients'. We can speculate that, if Heron's six categories of intervention are relevant to managers working with teachers, they are relevant in a different but parallel way for teachers working with students, not least because a teacher's main job is to provide support and learning opportunities.

The following sections will consider the first three steps in defining teacher development needs as a part of a cyclical process outlined in Figure 4.3. The cycle offers a logical and iterative sequence of steps which need to be gone through in order to ensure that professional development and learning are purposeful and, at

Assessing teachers' development needs

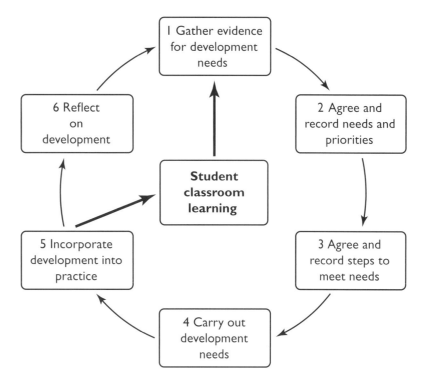

Figure 4.3 Teacher development cycle

the same time, relevant to the individual teachers, and so that teacher development leads to development in professional practice that improves the quality and effectiveness of teaching, and therefore benefits students' learning.

Gathering evidence for development needs

The word 'needs' has featured frequently in the paragraphs as well as in Figure 4.3. As with any kind of learning, establishing 'needs' is a logical and important first step, but how can 'needs' be separated from 'wishes' or 'interests'? As professionals, individual teachers usually have ideas about what areas related to language teaching and what aspects of methodology they wish to explore further. There is likely to be a diversity of such wishes and interests, ranging from relevant research in second language acquisition, to the use of ICT in teaching, to aspects of language form and use, and to the use of specific types of media such as puppets and toys with very young learners, or video clips and poetry with older learners. On the other hand, it may not be so easy for teachers to identify in what areas they need to develop in order to make their teaching more effective from the point of view of students and their learning. These different areas of development needs are outlined in Figure 4.4, which implies that defining development needs and deciding what support should be offered for teacher development is not as simple as it sounds.

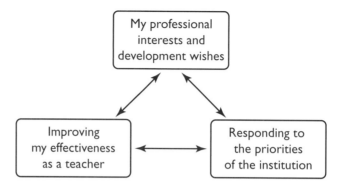

Figure 4.4 Competing or coinciding needs?

Activity 4.3 Prior to planning support for teacher development in an institution, what steps can be taken to identify and agree the development needs and wants of individual teachers, on the one hand, and of a teaching team, on the other?

The short answer can be expressed in three words: 'assessment', 'reflection', and 'discussion'. All three are needed at each angle of the triangle, and can take different forms in different institutions, and with different individuals.

Measures of effectiveness

In the USA, the Bill and Melinda Gates Foundation ran a three-year project between 2009 and 2012 called Measures of Effective Teaching (MET). It involved about 3,000 K–12 teachers of different subjects in various US locations. The aim was to find ways of assessing or evaluating the effectiveness of teaching that would be considered useful by teachers themselves and could result in improvements that would have an impact on students' learning (see Website references for more information about the project). In the 2013 project publication *Ensuring Fair and Reliable Measures of Effective Teaching*, an account is given of the studies carried out, first to determine whether 'effective teaching' makes a difference to student learning, and secondly how different ways of measuring effective teaching can be combined to be fairer and more reliable than single measures. Aspects of this project, whatever its lasting outcomes, are relevant to the question of assessing development needs. The measures focused on were of three main types: lesson observation of various kinds, feedback from students, and the results achieved by students on standardized tests. However, the main conclusion of the project was that the measures are fairer and more reliable if combined, and that they can be combined with different weightings to take account of varying external factors. We will return to the question of effectiveness in Chapter 8.

A key point arising from the MET project which is relevant to assessing development needs by whatever means is that it is useful to have concrete evidence to refer to, consider, and reflect on. Depending on the means of assessment, the evidence will take various forms, as indicated in Figure 4.5, which lists some of the main ways in which evidence can be gathered.

Types of evidence	Ways this evidence can be collected
Feedback from students (and their parents/carers, employers, etc.)	• Opinions gathered by questionnaire or focus group • Discussion with students, e.g. ranking of aspects of teaching from 'poor' to 'excellent' • Suggestions for change made by students and their sponsors • Quantitative analysis of these opinions and suggestions
Teaching observation	• Accounts of what happened • Checklists or notes of positive and less positive features • Real recorded data that can be separately analysed
Standardized tests of students' language ability	• Test results in quantitative and/or qualitative form • Examples of students' oral and/or written language
Self-assessment carried out by teachers against specified criteria	• Profiles showing areas where teachers believe their competences (knowledge and skills) are strong and not so strong
Teachers' own reports/diaries; surveys of teachers' opinions; discussions with the team	• Mainly subjective views of teachers' individual development needs and preferences; a majority view, possibly coloured by dominant individuals

Source: MET project 2012, © 2012 Bill & Melinda Gates Foundation

Figure 4.5 Some sources of evidence for defining teacher development needs

Activity 4.4 Look at Figure 4.5. Put the types of evidence listed in order of usefulness for helping to assess the development needs of individual teachers.

As mentioned above, an important principle of the MET project was that using a single source of evidence from one type of assessment is not as reliable or informative as drawing on more than one source of evidence. An advantage of teacher self-assessment, based on a tool such as the EPG, is that it can provide a structured, if still subjective, overview of where individual teachers feel their competences are strong and not so strong. If this is combined with regular observation by an LCM, the self-assessment can be verified, and development needs that take both sources of evidence into account can be agreed. If the views of students obtained through some kind of structured survey can also be taken into account, this will make the evidence stronger, but this evidence may not be consistent with the evidence gathered from self-assessment and from observation. For example, students may not pick up on points that the teacher and the LCM agree are important, but might point to other issues that are important to students, such as being corrected consistently and frequently.

Agreeing and recording needs and priorities

Bearing in mind the key role that teachers should have in managing their own development, the assessment of these needs should be a joint undertaking, but assessment alone is not sufficient. In order for there to be agreement, the needs have to be reflected on and described in a way that both the teacher and the LCM can relate to and follow up on. As an example, after one or more observations and watching recorded clips, it may be clear that student learning would be better supported if the teacher used a wider range of techniques for handling errors, rather than simply correcting students and moving on. Even though the teacher can understand from the observer's remarks and the evidence that something needs to be done, the development aim needs to be expressed clearly and positively. For example, the following description of the aims could be agreed in discussion between the teacher and LCM:

- reflect on and decide when correction of students' oral language is useful (and when it is less useful)
- select and try out some other techniques (in addition to correction by the teacher) for giving feedback and handling errors in oral work, including, for example, prompting students to correct themselves and eliciting suggested corrections from other students
- identify and put into practice ways of reinforcing correct language by giving clear models, eliciting repetition of these from students, and eliciting additional examples.

Writing such aims down in the record of the observation and/or in the **teacher's log** (see Chapter 5) is a way of ensuring that they are clear and agreed, and that they can be followed up.

Agreeing and recording steps to meet these needs

The discussion should also cover how the teacher can move towards these developmental aims, independently or with support.

Activity 4.5 — What, in your view, could the teacher do to make progress towards the aims outlined above? What support might they need from the institution?

Even where these fairly precise aims are concerned, several options can be suggested and agreed on, depending on the institutional context and the teacher's own circumstances:

- Reading relevant chapters in teachers' handbooks, such as Ur's discussion of correction (Ur, 2012, chapter 7) and Harmer's section on feedback during oral work (Harmer, 2007, pp. 142–147). This presupposes that teachers have access to books of this kind; if this is not the case, the institution will need to invest in a teachers' library, however small, and subscribe to relevant professional journals.

- Observation of, or team-teaching with, teachers who already use a wider range of techniques for handling errors (recorded clips of teaching can be useful here). This requires that the teacher is available or can be substituted to take part in such observation or team-teaching.
- Participating in discussion with colleagues, especially with the teacher they have observed or want to observe, about different approaches to and techniques for giving feedback and handling errors. This could be part of a regular meeting organized by the institution.
- Invited observation by a **mentor** or peer who is asked to focus and comment on how the teacher gives feedback and handles errors. This presupposes that time is allowed for peer observation and/or that there is a mentoring scheme (see Chapter 7).

The many different ways in which teachers can autonomously develop their competences and be supported in their development will be explored in more detail in Chapter 5. As will be discussed in Chapter 6, writing down development steps like those above and, if possible, indicating when the steps can be taken provides a basis for reporting and reflection on development, and follow-up discussion with the manager, perhaps before further observation.

A flexible approach

While the LCM, together with other managers, is responsible for implementing the institution's policies, the team as a whole needs to feel that they have a say in the details and the manner of implementation. In other words, there needs to be an ongoing two-way process of engagement from the beginning in setting up and agreeing priorities and development activities, and when these should be reviewed and further steps agreed. Without being simplistic, an easy guide is how evenly dialogue is shared between teachers and the LCM in group and one-to-one meetings, including feedback on observation (see Chapter 7) or consultations about INSET development workshops. If the observer/LCM is talking more than the members of staff or the observed teacher, the dialogue is probably less valuable and team spirit may be adversely affected.

LCMs need to demonstrate that they too are reflecting on their work and seeking to develop. For example, LCMs who also teach can assess themselves and talk about areas where they feel they can improve, and so encourage others to self-assess and reflect on their work. LCMs can also record some of their own teaching, discuss the recordings with some teachers, and invite feedback, thereby encouraging self-recording, sharing, and openness. In general terms, inviting feedback on the way you manage people can be valuable in relationship building as well as useful in raising managers' self-awareness. This can be done occasionally in individual interactions as well as in the context of individual performance review meetings, which will be discussed in Chapter 7.

Conclusion

In this chapter, the important process of defining and agreeing development needs and discussing how they can be worked on has been explored. The emphasis has been on a shared process outlined in stages 1, 2, and 3 of the teacher development cycle depicted in Figure 4.3 (see page 51), in which the responsibility of teachers for their own development is not undermined but supported by the LCM, while the institution's own requirements and the whole teaching team's needs are also considered. By going through these processes, LCMs have a good chance of ensuring that individual professional development is, and is felt to be, relevant and of a high quality. This will in turn contribute to the effectiveness of teaching and the quality of learning. The following chapter will look at the remaining three steps of the teacher development cycle.

5 SUPPORTING AND MONITORING TEACHERS' PROFESSIONAL DEVELOPMENT

Introduction

Chapter 4 emphasized the importance of identifying the diverse development needs of teachers within an institution and also of considering the needs and profile of the whole team. These areas correspond to steps 1, 2, and 3 of the teacher development cycle which was presented in the last chapter, and is shown again below in Figure 5.1. This chapter is concerned with the role of the institution and its LCM in developing and implementing a systematic but flexible approach to supporting teacher development that has an impact on professional practice in the classroom and beyond, and on teacher effectiveness, and is recorded and reflected on by the teacher. These areas are represented in steps 4, 5, and 6 of the teacher development cycle.

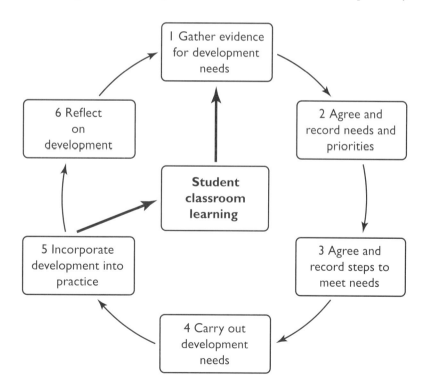

Figure 5.1 Teacher development cycle

Supporting teacher development

As was emphasized earlier in this book, and in *Language Teaching Competences*, a guiding principle is that teacher development should be under the control of individual teachers. This use of 'development' is not interpersonal in that LCMs and the institution do the developing: instead, it implies that teachers themselves develop their awareness and skills, and their general competence as language teachers. The role of the institution and its LCMs is to support and guide that development. This support and guidance can take many forms, but it should, in the end, be based on the motivation and consent of individual teachers.

Activity 5.1

In your experience as a teacher and/or as an LCM, which of the activities and events in Figure 5.2 have contributed most to teacher development? List the top four in order of importance. Then chose the top two that, in your opinion, have caused the most concern or upset among teachers.

> 1 Lesson observation by an LCM with a follow-up discussion
> 2 Short observations by an LCM or external agency without feedback
> 3 Observation by peers/colleagues with a follow-up discussion
> 4 **Self-observation** – recording oneself teaching and watching/listening to it alone or with an LCM or colleague
> 5 Observing colleagues and discussing the observation with them
> 6 Team-teaching – sharing a class with a colleague (i.e. two teachers in the room)
> 7 Tandem teaching – sharing a class with a colleague over a period of time (i.e. joint planning and discussion, one teacher in the room at a time)
> 8 INSET workshops on topics selected by the institution
> 9 INSET workshops on topics selected in consultation with teachers
> 10 Leading a workshop as a teacher
> 11 Attending external conferences or workshops with financial support from the institution and reporting back to colleagues on the event
> 12 Participating as a speaker in an external workshop or conference
> 13 Discussing classroom teaching ideas informally with colleagues
> 14 Working with colleagues on materials, online resources, tests, a course programme, etc.
> 15 Being involved in a **classroom research** project (e.g. trying out new techniques or materials and collecting data on the impact)
> 16 Being involved in a reading group with colleagues (e.g. looking at different articles on the same topic and discussing them)
> 17 Preparing for and beginning to teach a course or level that is new to the teacher
> 18 Mentoring a less experienced or newly appointed colleague
> 19 Being involved in coordination (e.g. coordinating classes at the same level)
> 20 Self-assessment against a list of competence criteria or **descriptors** such as those in the EPG
> 21 Discussing feedback on teaching with one's own students
> 22 Other activities not included in this list

Figure 5.2 Some options for supporting teacher development

The list in Figure 5.2, which is not intended to be comprehensive, illustrates the wide range of activities, events, and challenges that can potentially contribute to a teacher's professional development. However, whether any such activity actually does contribute to professional growth, even in a small way, depends on numerous factors, some to do with the individual teacher and their previous experiences, career history, attitudes, and state of mind, and some related to the context – for example, whether the activity is voluntary or obligatory, whether sufficient time is available, who else is involved, and so on. Of course, much also depends on the way the activity, event, or experience is carried out, supported, and managed.

Teacher development should not be a low priority: it is so important to the well-being of the institution and of teachers and their students' learning that a strategic approach is required in order for it to be effective. As Wei et al. (2009, p. 3) point out:

> While the impact on student achievement is a critical indicator of the effectiveness of professional development, we believe the impact of professional development on teacher knowledge and instructional practice is also relevant, as these are worthwhile outcomes in themselves that support increased learning for students.

Providing effective support for teacher development involves specifying clear objectives and putting in place one or more systems, as well as actions that then need to be backed up with resources, both human and financial. The systems need to be based on the mission and values of the institution and to be responsive to the needs and development both of individual teachers and of the team as a whole. In the next part of this chapter we will explore step 4 of the teacher development cycle from two perspectives: development activities for the whole teaching team and for individual teachers.

Development steps for the whole teaching team

Apart from assisting teachers, however experienced and confident they are, to meet their individual professional development needs and wants, institutions should also make provisions for professional development activities that can involve the whole teaching team, or subgroups of teachers within the team. As well as adding a dimension to professional development for individual teachers, such activities can have an important incremental impact on team spirit and collegiality by providing opportunities for professional interaction among team members of a kind that is not normally possible in the short intervals before, between, and after teaching duties, when the priorities are likely to be last-minute preparation and 'having a break'.

Activity 5.2	In your experience, what kinds of professional development activities involving some or all members of a teaching team can be organized in educational institutions? In your opinion, which of these is most likely to contribute to professional development, and which is most likely to contribute to team building and team spirit?

The following activities are common or have been reported on:
- INSET and development workshops on a given topic or theme, either as stand-alone events or as part of a series on the same general theme
- online INSET events organized by the institution in the form of webinars or podcasts
- teachers' conference organized as a one-day event or longer, e.g. before the beginning of the academic year
- short courses on a given topic run by the institution, say 12 hours spread over six weeks on a morning or afternoon when teaching does not take place, or as part of a staff conference
- similar courses made available online, e.g. via Moodle (see Website references)
- informal face-to-face discussion and reading groups, where a theme is chosen and relevant reading material is identified for individuals to read and comment on
- online forums for teachers in an institution
- project work involving a small team, e.g. to develop supplementary materials for a given age group or level or on a given theme, or progress tests, etc.
- classroom-based research or **action research**, in which a small group of teachers explore questions about teaching and learning by collecting and analysing data from classrooms.

Of these, INSET workshops are probably the most common but may have a low impact on teacher development, especially if the topics are decided by LCMs without consultation and they are one-off events. This brings us back to the need for a coherent, thought-through approach to group development activities. Borg (2016), whose research has explored the area of teacher cognition and professional development in some depth, has commented on the lack of impact of most INSET. Reviewing recent literature on INSET across the curriculum, Borg argues that its impact is limited because:
- it is often seen by the institution and its LCMs as an 'administrative formality'
- it does not respond to well-defined needs
- the topics are identified by someone outside the teaching team
- it is infrequent and short-term – more a series of events than a process
- it is input-based, implying priority being given to 'received knowledge'
- it is not followed up.

Borg concludes that effective INSET needs to be teacher-led, ongoing, school-based, collaborative and social, and needs to involve reflection and inquiry and contribute to **professional learning**.

There is food for thought here for all institutions and LCMs that provide regular—for example, weekly or monthly—workshops for their teaching teams focusing on different topics. The questions that need to be answered, whatever approach is adopted to planning and providing INSET for the team, are commented on in Figure 5.3.

How often should INSET activities be organized, and at what time of the week?	This will depend to a significant extent on whether attendance of all or a certain number of such activities is part of the contract, i.e. is remunerated. This is an especially sensitive area for hourly paid teachers, whose remuneration is generally calculated on the basis of the number of hours taught. Institutions need to take a strategic approach to this question.
Should they be obligatory or voluntary?	This will also depend on the contract. If participation is a requirement of the contract, motivation among teachers may be reduced. If Borg's effectiveness criteria are not met, voluntary attendance may mean that some teachers almost never participate in these events, yet they may be the very people that would most benefit. In addition, some of the activities listed earlier, such as reading and discussion groups or classroom research, would not work well if the whole team participated.
Who should decide on form and content?	Consultation is an absolute necessity, especially when LCMs have a clear agenda on which they wish to focus. Teachers need to feel they have a leading role to play in deciding on INSET, so the more consensus among teachers about the nature, content, and format of such activities, the more likely they are to participate enthusiastically and benefit from them.
Who should lead or run INSET activities?	Depending on the topic, LCMs may not have the experience or expertise to run all of them, and leading or co-leading INSET activities is itself a development opportunity for teachers. Once the topics and format are agreed with the team, inviting teachers to run a majority of them is a good way of recognizing specific expertise within the team. However, the time spent preparing them may need to be remunerated in some way.
Should the activities be targeted at the whole team or at subgroups within the team?	Given the likely diversity of expertise and experience across a teaching team, it is unlikely that activities such as workshops will be felt to be useful to all. Workshops can be targeted at subgroups, for example those with only initial qualifications, or those teaching certain types of course. Or there can be a mixed approach: some teachers are asked to be involved in some activities, while for others, involvement is voluntary. As discussed, some activities will only work if small groups are involved.
How can INSET be 'ongoing'?	One-off short activities like isolated workshops or talks from invited speakers need to be the exception. Professional learning involves teachers focusing on an issue that concerns and interests them in more than one activity over time, and to have opportunities to relate it to their classroom practice.
What records should be kept?	The institution should keep a careful record of the activities it has organized or supported, and who has participated. Teachers who participate can be asked to keep their own records in their teacher's logs.

Figure 5.3 Practical aspects of providing INSET activities

Logistics

One of the challenges in educational institutions is to find time and space in the busy week for CPD activities. Some institutions construct a timetable that leaves a morning or an afternoon free, while others schedule them after teaching is completed or in breaks between teaching where there is a gap in the middle of the day between morning and evening courses. Then there are the issues of diverse timetables and multiple locations which are especially problematic for institutions which offer language courses in the corporate sector or have contracts with mainstream schools. If teachers spend part of their time away from the institution's main premises, it is especially difficult for them to participate in collective activities in person. A solution that is becoming increasingly common for such institutions and those which have branches in various locations is to use an online means of organizing CPD. While these do not usually allow the same kinds of interaction within the team, except via ancillary chat messages, forum posts, tweets, etc., they can enable teachers to participate in CPD events outside working hours at a time convenient to them. Single events can take the form of videoconferences which, depending on the application used, allow up to 25 participants in different locations to communicate via mobile devices or computers in real time. For example, an institution can set up a webinar—an online seminar—for its teachers, in which they explore a certain topic. Although this allows for geographical flexibility, the institution still needs to select a specific time to allow for oral interaction during the webinar. Webinars are also likely to be focused on 'input', although the person leading the webinar can include pauses for tasks. Publishers and other institutions involved in language education regularly offer such webinars. It can be seen, however, that such online events alone would not be a sufficient response to development needs like developing techniques for handling errors, discussed in Chapter 4.

Development steps for individual teachers

An important point is that teacher development is 'a continuing process of becoming and can never be finished' (Mann, 2005, p. 105). In other words, no teachers, however experienced, should think that their professional development is somehow complete, even if the kinds and the means of development needed are different from those appropriate to less experienced teachers, and even if the means of responding to these needs are not normally available in the institution. The challenge for LCMs is to find ways of encouraging experienced teachers to think about their further development, and to identify ways of supporting that ongoing development effectively.

In reality, no development system works perfectly for every teacher, since each individual has differing needs and will develop in different ways. In a system that seeks to cater for diverse individual needs, several tools and mechanisms are required to ensure that it is as effective as possible. These include, for example, a menu of options or steps for development, and a means of planning and implementing these activities such as:

- a scheme for mentoring teachers who require ongoing support
- individual teacher's logs for recording agreed development objectives and proposed steps (discussed in more detail later in this chapter)
- an institutional record covering the development objectives and steps of all team members
- a means of acknowledging teachers' development efforts and progress.

Activity 5.3 Imagine that you are managing a team of 12 well-motivated teachers, most of whom have only limited experience, and two of whom are very experienced. The Director of the institution has promised that a significant sum of money will be made available to support individual teacher development. Looking back at the list in Figure 5.2 (see page 58), consider which options you would prioritize, and which of these would need to be budgeted for.

Not all the possibilities outlined in Figure 5.2 are necessarily suitable for supporting individual teacher development. For example, workshops need to cater for a group, and attending conferences may be useful but may not directly correspond to agreed development needs. The options can be divided into groups:

- activities related to observation of lessons, including being observed, observing others, and self-observation
- activities involving working with a colleague, such as team-teaching or mentoring
- new kinds of professional experience, such as teaching a new kind of course or taking on a new responsibility
- autonomous activities, including self-assessment and reflection but also reading and experimentation.

Of these, only the first two are likely to require targeted resources in addition to management time: 'observation' implies that someone with the relevant experience is available to carry out the observation, and perhaps that a teacher needs to be substituted so that they can observe specific lessons. Working with others can also have financial implications if it includes being mentored, since the mentors may be teachers who need to be released from some of their teaching duties. In addition, team-teaching and peer observation requiring two teachers in the same classroom is likely to be costly unless the teacher seeking development is available to team-teach or observe a peer in his or her own time. However, the financial burden could be reduced by making the team-teaching, peer observation, and the mentoring short-term for a fixed period of time, rather than open-ended. Also, most teachers are willing to invest some of their own time in professional development if they believe it is useful and beneficial both to their students and to themselves.

Activity 5.4 At the same institution described in Activity 5.3, a less experienced teacher is having difficulty planning her lessons in a realistic way and then implementing the plan in class. She finds it hard to manage the students and finds herself struggling to keep their concentration. As a consequence, she hardly ever gets through what she has planned, and the class is falling behind compared to other classes working on the same course programme. Following observation, you have both agreed that the development focus needs to be on managing learning activities, and on time management. What development steps would you try to agree with this teacher?

This is a case where mentoring, preferably also involving some team-teaching and observation, would be desirable. Quite often, development of this kind involves 'unlearning' certain habits acquired during one's teaching experience. If a mentor is able to support the teacher for, say, two hours each week for a month, a productive one-to-one relationship can develop in which, for example, the mentor combines some or all of the following activities:

- short recorded observations of the teacher followed by discussion of the recordings and practical suggestions
- observation of the mentor's class by the teacher, followed by discussion
- jointly planned team-teaching, in which the teacher takes over certain activities in one of the mentor's lesson, and the results reviewed
- further observation by the mentor of one of the teacher's lessons, in which she tries to replicate and adapt the techniques learned from observation and team-teaching.

Observing lessons or recordings of lessons given by other teachers, and having an organized feedback session with students, are other activities that could be considered. However, it must be emphasized that such support for development will work best if the teacher in question has a say in how the support is organized, and has opportunities both to express his or her feelings in confidence and to actively learn from peers, especially the mentor. Mentoring is explored in more detail in the following section.

Mentoring schemes

Mentoring schemes were made popular in UK mainstream education in the late 20th century because they provided a way for schools to provide help to teachers who needed it without appointing more academic management staff or bringing in trainers. A big advantage is that mentors can provide both direct support for professional development, as well as encourage and help their **mentees** to put their professional learning into practice in the classroom. Let us consider again the needs identified in Activity 5.4. The teacher concerned may have undertaken various development steps such as observing other teachers and reading about planning and class management. The mentor supporting her can help with planning, for example, by going over a lesson plan and asking questions about why activities are in the order chosen, or about how the teacher will move from one activity to the next. Afterwards, the mentor can observe the teacher's lesson and discuss with her to what extent the learning was incorporated into practice, and, in the role of a coach, make suggestions about how to improve further. This is why it is so important for mentors and mentees to have an ongoing relationship. The mentoring need not last for months, but there needs to be time for the mentor and mentee to work together alternately on the ongoing development of the mentee's awareness and practical skills, and on seeing how they are incorporated into professional practice in the classroom. This involves mixing direct guidance and support at all stages: planning, focused observation, feedback, and discussion. Needless to say, the fact that each mentee has different needs means that mentoring can be a rich learning experience for the mentor as well.

The roles and responsibilities of mentors

The precise responsibilities of mentors in a given institution, and the ways used to select and orientate them, require careful consideration. In principle, mentors are peers rather than supervisors or coordinators, although in some institutions with large numbers of teachers, LCMs and supervisors may share the mentoring role. As colleagues, mentors are perhaps easier to relate to for less experienced teachers and teachers with specific developmental needs. Their role is to provide both moral and practical support without trying to persuade their mentees of a particular approach to teaching. If the mentor also has management duties, these two roles need to be kept separate. It is more important for mentees to be encouraged to teach in their own way, and to learn how to do this effectively, than to be told how to work. The implication is that not all experienced teachers are suitable mentors.

Activity 5.5

You have agreed with the teacher from Activity 5.4 that it would be beneficial to find her a mentor to help develop her management of learning activities and improve her lesson planning. Using a table like the one below, make a list of the essential and desirable experience/qualities you think the mentor will need.

	Essential	**Desirable**
Experience as a teacher		
Other experience		
Personal characteristics		

As discussed above, each teacher will have different developmental needs so a mentor's role will also vary from mentee to mentee. In their book, *Teaching Teachers*, Malderez & Wedell (2007) list a number of potential roles for mentors of teachers. These include:

- Acculturator: helping the mentee to adjust to a new institution
- Model: modelling enthusiasm for learning ... attitudes to peers, learners and parents/carers, rather than modelling ways of teaching
- Support: a shoulder to cry on or a listening ear, for which a close and trusting relationship is needed
- Sponsor: someone who can intercede on behalf of the mentee, for example, to obtain teaching materials through the LCM
- Educator: helping mentees to articulate, reflect on, and improve their understanding of what goes on in the classroom.

(Adapted from Malderez & Wedell, 2007, pp. 86–87)

Combining these roles successfully from the point of view of respective mentees requires skill, experience, and empathy, as well as a perceptive approach to the various needs of teachers with different backgrounds and personalities. Mentors need sufficient experience as teachers to be able to advise and support those they are asked to mentor. For example, if a teacher is learning how to cope effectively with teenage students having had little experience with this age group, it is important that the mentor has had successful experience with teenagers – and views that experience as positive. Importantly, the mentor also needs to have had experience of collaborating with colleagues in different ways: team-teaching and even providing good feedback on observation may be hard to do well if the mentor has never done it before. Perhaps most importantly, the mentor needs to have excellent interpersonal skills and to be able to work with colleagues with different personalities. Sensitivity, an ability to listen, and an ability to look at teaching situations from different perspectives are invaluable qualities.

As mentioned previously, mentors are usually appointed by LCMs for a fixed period of time, especially when a less experienced colleague or indeed anyone new begins work at the institution, because the mentor can play an invaluable role helping staff to adapt to new systems and a different way of working as well as providing pedagogic support. Teachers selected as mentors are frequently released from some of their teaching to allow time for them to work with one or more colleagues. See Figure 5.4 for a typical list of what mentors' responsibilities might look like.

Incorporating professional learning into practice

A key stage in the teacher development cycle is the gradual implementation of learning into professional practice in the classroom and, where appropriate, beyond. Individual teachers have to take responsibility for this but they can be encouraged and supported in several ways.

Supporting and monitoring teachers' professional development 67

> **Guidelines for mentors**
>
> **Induction**
>
> When meeting the mentee(s) for the first time, ensure that they fully understand how the curriculum and syllabus work. Assist mentees by going through the teachers' handbook with them and:
>
> - showing them where supplementary materials, teachers' resources, tests, and so on are kept
> - orientating them to resources stored online and to ICT facilities available to teachers
> - answering questions about the timetable and who is responsible for what.
>
> **Support**
>
> When development needs have been defined and agreed (usually with an LCM), discuss them briefly with the mentee(s), and work out with them detailed plans of support. Typical kinds of support may include:
>
> - discussing lesson plans and mentees' concerns about students, the materials specified in the course programme, and any other aspect of the classes assigned to them
> - observing their lessons, followed by discussion and advice on specific aspects, primarily those included among the development objectives, and also other issues (if time is available)
> - inviting them to observe relevant parts of some of your own lessons and, depending on the skills being worked on, inviting them to plan and share the teaching of a relevant lesson with you.
>
> **Reporting**
>
> Half-way through and at the end of the mentoring period, you will be asked to provide a brief progress report. This report should be discussed with the mentee(s) and should include your own comments and recommendations for further action and support.

Figure 5.4 A typical list of mentoring guidelines

Activity 5.6

A relatively inexperienced teacher has been reading articles about the teaching of pronunciation and has also attended two workshops on the topic. Up to now, he has mainly relied on correction and repetition of pronunciation points when they arise in class. He would now like to start implementing a more systematic approach. There are few pronunciation exercises in the textbook, so he needs to get some help and advice. What kind of help would be most useful?

There are many possibilities for the teacher in Activity 5.6. These include looking for a supplementary coursebook that focuses on pronunciation and photocopying/ adapting exercises from it, and creating some materials of his own. For example, he could use flash cards of objects and/or animals that involve similar but different sounds, and also audio and video clips, that could be used in listening and elicitation exercises, and in interactive practice. As he is a relatively inexperienced teacher, he could get some help and advice by:

- showing his proposed plan for class activities involving these materials to a more experienced colleague or his mentor if he has one
- asking his students why they thought they had done the exercises and whether they found them useful.

Having his mentor or a colleague observe him while he tries out one or more of the activities, or recording himself if this isn't possible, would be useful in assessing how well it went. Keeping a note in his teacher's log of what went well and what didn't really work could also help. Even without observation or recording, being able to review and discuss with a colleague how the implementation has worked out is likely to be helpful and lead to suggestions and further ideas.

A key point is that implementation is unlikely to work perfectly the first time: it is a gradual process, and often part of a longer period of experimentation. For example, in this case, having successfully implemented some ideas for practising the sounds of the language, a further step could be to implement ways of practising sentence stress and rhythm involving whole utterances, and also, or later, intonation. Each new implementation will not only activate prior learning derived from discussion, observation, and reading, but will itself contribute to learning by experience, becoming gradually more confident and creative through a process of experimentation and self-monitoring.

Reflecting on development

As can be seen from Activity 5.6, reflecting on one's own learning and the development of one's practice is an essential part of the process. Although this is the sixth step in the teacher development cycle depicted in Figure 5.1 (see page 57), it is important to note that it is not the final one but rather the beginning of a new cycle. As well as helping to decide how successful implementation has been from both the learners' and the teacher's point of view, it is also a means of identifying whether more help and support is needed, in what area, and what form of help would be most useful. For teacher development activities to have a lasting impact, it is essential for the teacher concerned to articulate the development that they have experienced, including the benefits and the changes noticed in their teaching. This step helps teachers to take the learning on board in a personal, meaningful way. It is also important for the institution and LCM as it provides a record of what activities took place and what their impact was, which in turn can help inform future professional development strategy.

Teacher's logs

A teacher's log is a kind of diary in any form that is kept up to date by each individual teacher. It should include details of the teacher's development objectives or priorities (these will be the priorities agreed with the teacher's immediate supervisor or the LCM) for a given period, say three or six months, but also other development aims that the teacher might add or that might be triggered later on. Linked to these objectives, the teacher's log should contain some actions that have been agreed and, when decided, the timescale or dates of these. Following each development step, there should be space for some reflection: how did the lesson/day go? What impact has it had, if any, on classroom practice and student learning? Are there implications for the next step?

Once the procedure has been agreed with teachers, the template for the teacher's log could be negotiated with teachers and then provided by the LCM, so that each teacher is using the same format, making it easier for the LCM to keep track. Figure 5.5 is an example of a teacher's log with entries by the teacher in Activity 5.4 (on page 64). The log can be filled in either electronically or on paper, although an electronic version is more easily shared.

Development aims	Agreed actions	Deadline	Reflection
Improve lesson planning – needs to be more realistic and varied	Work with J [mentor] on this: 20 mins per week	February–March	Really helpful – J so practical Plans much simpler and less ambitious now
Improve management of lesson activities, especially changing, grouping, etc.	Team-teach with J once weekly – co-planning and managing alternate activities	March	Worked brilliantly – feeling so much more confident, and learning a lot from the way J handles the activities
Learn more about student motivation and attention	Read chapter 3 in X and article given to me by LCM	March	Useful, especially about different learning styles and 'intrinsic' motivation Found another article in X Workshop on motivation organized by school was also relevant – I'm not the only one with problems, and others had good suggestions to offer
Work on keeping students focused and improving motivation	Get J to observe one of my lessons each week (will record if possible)	April	First lesson a disaster, but J's comments and suggestions helped a lot – have to be firmer with disruptive students Next lesson went a bit better – J and I watched video together and he pointed out things in my body language and voice I wasn't aware of

Figure 5.5 *Possible layout of a teacher's log*

It is important that teachers also include new development aims that have occurred to them independently of any assessment or discussion with others, and any related activities. Autonomous self-motivated development is as valuable as the more structured negotiated development agreed on with the LCM, but it may be focused on issues that are especially important to the individual teacher and may, therefore, be less related to institutional concerns. The institution may not, for example, believe that dictation is of much value in modern language education, but if a teacher finds it useful and motivating for learners and decides to develop his or her knowledge and skills in this area, it may lead not only to improved job satisfaction but also to a reappraisal within the team of the usefulness of this technique for student learning. Indeed, the teacher may find herself running a workshop on the topic.

Institutional records

If teacher's logs can be shared with LCMs and mentors, the tracking of individual development is much easier. What LCMs need is an overview of the agreed development aims of each individual teacher, and what each of them is focusing on. This enables LCMs to:

- identify teachers with similar or overlapping development needs, which could be useful when appointing mentors and planning joint development actions
- keep track of how each teacher is developing and update the team profile so that it can be taken into account when deciding which classes to assign to them in future
- propose collective professional development activities that are relevant to the needs and interests of several teachers.

LCMs are likely to have an electronic or paper-based folder for each teacher in which the teacher's logs can be kept alongside the periodic self-assessments that they may have done based on a competence framework like the EPG, records of the classes they have taught, and notes on appraisals or professional development reviews (see Chapter 8). In addition, LCMs can create a simple overview of the team as a whole, starting with competence profiles like those generated by the e-Grid version of the EPG (see Website references), current development objectives, and other data, for example feedback from students, participation in workshops and non-teaching activities, and so on. Participation in group INSET and professional development activities and projects should also be recorded.

Recognition of development progress

There is little doubt that teacher development will be more enthusiastically engaged in and probably more effective if progress is formally, as well as informally, acknowledged in some way. How this is done will depend on various factors, including whether the institution has or participates in some formal scheme, and what the recognition consists of.

Key questions to be considered first are: what do we mean by 'progress' in this context, how can progress best be assessed, and by whom? Progress implies that teachers are moving forward in their development aims, and that changes in their actual teaching are perceptible to themselves and to observers. This brings us back to measuring effective teaching, in which observation plays an important role (including observation by mentors). Students' feedback and student learning, i.e. the results of student assessments, are also useful sources of evidence. Other evidence may include teachers' own feelings: do they now feel more confident and comfortable with the aspects of their teaching that they have been focusing on? Is their progress reflected in their own self-assessment, which could be related to specific criteria or indicators like those suggested in the Eaquals Framework for Language Teacher Training and Development (see Website references)? It is important that, however they are gauged, the nature and degree of the progress achieved is discussed and agreed between individual teachers and the LCM.

Activity 5.7   In your experience, what form can an institution's recognition of individual teachers' progress take? What kinds of recognition are likely to be most appreciated by and most useful to teachers?

An obvious answer from a teacher's point of view might be financial recognition, but the practical difficulties of a system which reliably measures this kind of progress make concrete links between teacher development and pay problematic. Some institutions, for example, use a points system related to teachers' completion of certain INSET courses: accumulating points over a period (usually at least a year) can move teachers into a different band on the pay scale or entitle them to certain rewards such as being able to attend an external conference at the institution's expense.

At the very least, recognition can be shown in writing through a brief written report describing the development steps taken and the progress made. This can be especially valuable to teachers who work at the institution only for a fixed period and then leave because work is no longer available or for other reasons. An official report which is dated can be a useful supplement to a CV.

Conclusion

This chapter has explored ways in which individual and group professional development can be supported by the institution that teachers work for following the teacher development cycle shown in Figure 5.1. Each teacher, even those on part-time or fixed-term contracts, needs to have a set of realistic professional development aims for a defined period of time. These aims are arrived at following steps 1 to 3 in the cycle. The LCM's job is to help the teacher to define and act on these aims without disempowering the teacher (steps 3 and 4). In addition, also as a result of steps 1 to 3, opportunities need to be identified to encourage the teaching team to participate in ongoing and varied INSET and professional development activities that cater to their collective needs and interests and enable them to build on one another's knowledge, skills, and interests, in a community of practice (step 4). The challenge for LCMs is to establish a system that functions well given the constraints on teachers' time and preoccupations, and to foster a climate that encourages professional development that is effective from all stakeholders' points of view, including the students'. Perhaps most important of all, depending on the development that has been engaged in, is the follow-through: helping and encouraging teachers to incorporate their learning in some way in their professional practice, to record their experiences, and to reflect constructively on this implementation and what further development steps they may need and wish to take (steps 5 and 6).

Chapter 6 will focus on classroom observation, a topic that has come up in both this and the previous chapter. It is a powerful management and development tool with great potential as a means of identifying development priorities and supporting the development of experienced teachers, as well as the training of those who are new to language teaching. In different ways it is relevant to all steps of the teacher development cycle and, for this reason, we will explore the topic in a chapter of its own.

6 OBSERVING TEACHERS IN THE CLASSROOM

Introduction

Lesson observation has been mentioned at various points in Chapters 4 and 5 because it has a key role to play in different stages of the teacher development cycle as well as in the pre-service training of teachers.

Observation has an obvious role to play in teacher training courses, especially when teaching practice is an integral part of the training programme and a central focus for some of the coursework. Observation is also an important and quite controversial part of an LCM's work. Much has been written about its benefits and disadvantages, and different ways of making classroom observation more valuable from the serving teacher's point of view. Indeed, it is potentially so valuable that it is incumbent upon institutions and their managers to find ways of making it work well from the point of view of all stakeholders. To achieve this, at least the following questions need to be considered carefully and answered clearly:

- What useful functions can lesson observations perform?
- Who carries them out? At least two or three different categories of staff could be observing lessons.
- What procedures are used, and have the teachers being observed agreed to them?
- What records are kept of observations, and do teachers who have been observed contribute to and agree with these?
- Is live recording used as part of observation? If so, for what purposes?
- What (if anything) happens as a consequence of observations?
- Where is the balance of control over observations between the observer or LCM and the teacher being observed?

Activity 6.1 Consider an observation system that you are familiar with, either as an LCM or as a teacher. How would you answer the questions above in relation to that particular system? On a scale of 1 to 5 (in which 5 equals very useful) rate the effectiveness of the system you are thinking of:
- from the typical teacher's point of view
- from the institution's point of view.

Key issues and guidelines relating to different ways of organizing and following up observation will be explored later in this chapter. The purpose of Activity 6.1 was to enable readers to focus their attention on the nature and quality of an **observation scheme** that they know and have perhaps experienced at first hand, and to reassess its effectiveness.

This chapter explores various types and aspects of lesson observation in greater detail, with a view to examining how observation can contribute to the goal of encouraging teacher development, and thereby enhance the quality and effectiveness of teaching and learning. It begins with a review of some key questions about observation and goes on to examine ways of organizing and conducting lesson observation for the purposes of assessing and identifying development needs and aiding the development of teacher competences and know-how.

Types of observation

Bailey (2006) draws a distinction between five types of observation. The types are more or less self-explanatory. At one extreme are 'surprise' or 'announced' observations, and at the other 'unseen' observations, where the observer is not present but discusses the teacher's own account of his or her lesson. It is noteworthy that between the two extremes are 'negotiated' observations, where the teacher and observer agree together on when and for how long observation should take place, and also 'invited' observations, where the observer responds to a request for observation. Bailey uses an interesting image to capture the differences between types of observation, as shown in Figure 6.1.

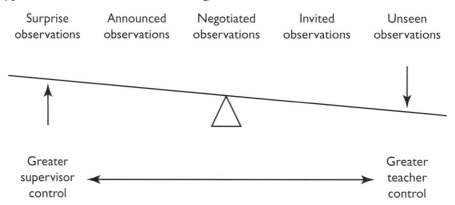

Source: *Language Teacher Supervision: A Case-Based Approach* (Cambridge Language Teaching Library) by Kathleen M Bailey, © Cambridge University Press 2006

Figure 6.1 *Supervisor (LCM) and teacher control over arranging classroom observation (Bailey, 2006, p. 85)*

Unseen observations are an interesting concept. Powell (1999) points to some of the advantages: apart from being time-effective, since the manager's presence in the classroom is not needed, some aspects such as lesson planning are, he believes, 'more susceptible to honest introspection than to observation' and are 'less judgmental; as a rule, description rather than prescription occurs, and this tends to generate more alternatives' (p. 3). Powell advocates a set procedure involving two questionnaires, one on general beliefs about teaching before the lesson, and the other on specific areas of teaching that is to be completed afterwards. It could be argued that, while such questionnaires may aid self-assessment, they are not strictly necessary. Teachers are often quite capable of recording the important points arising from a lesson if they have time to sit down and reflect. Teacher's logs are sometimes used for this purpose and as a diary in which teachers can note down feelings and insights after teaching.

A similar practice to unseen observations is self-observation. In this case, teachers record their lessons or parts of their lessons on video or audio equipment in order to be able to play the lesson back and review and reflect on exactly what happened. If done with a stationary camera or mobile device on a tripod, the recordings cannot capture everything but will enable teachers to remember the detail of what took place and to assess their own performance from different points of view. This can add a new dimension to unseen observations: instead of just filling out questionnaires, the teacher can select clips from the recording to discuss with the mentor.

Purposes and variables of lesson observation

Activity 6.2 Look at Figure 6.2 and consider the various purposes which lesson observation can serve in the first row of the table. Then for each column write notes on a piece of paper answering the questions in the left-hand column about how the observations should be organized to achieve these purposes.

Purpose of observation	Identifying a teacher's development needs	Supporting a teacher's development	Checking the quality of teaching and learning
Announced, unannounced, or negotiated?			
How explicit should focus be?			
Who can/should observe?			
Duration of observation?			
What preparatory steps desirable?			
What follow-up desirable?			

Figure 6.2 Variables in lesson observation

As can be seen from Activity 6.2, there are several variables in lesson observations, each of which has an impact both on the observed teacher and on the observer. Some of the variables depend on the type of observation as well as on the purpose. The main factors can be summarized as follows:

- Who is the observer? It could be the LCM, an external person, mentor, peer, or even the teacher him or herself.
- Is there a meeting or conversation beforehand?
- Is a plan given to the observer beforehand?
- Frequency of observation – is it the first time with this observer, one of a series, a follow-up, etc.?
- How long will the observation last (whole lesson, part of the lesson, etc.)?
- Is there any recording during the observation?
- Will the observer refer to specific criteria or focus points, for example in a checklist or form?
- Will there be a feedback discussion? If so, how soon after the observation?
- Will a written record of the observation and feedback be kept? If so, will it be given to and approved by the observed teacher?

In many institutions there is an established observation scheme, in some cases, covering observations of different kinds. Where this is the case, it is important for LCMs to think carefully through the above issues and to ensure that teachers understand the rationale of the observation types being used, and have a say in how they are organized. Teachers should also be involved in reviewing the way the scheme has been working, and whether changes are needed. Observations are much more likely to be productive and useful if teachers—as well as LCMs—can see the value of them, and if the control aspect of observations is well balanced between LCMs and teachers.

Maingay (1988) identifies four purposes of observation: for training, for development, for assessment, and for observer development. For Maingay, observation for training purposes takes place mainly during initial and INSET courses which include live teaching practice that can be observed by the trainers and also by other trainees. Observation for assessment purposes is also a feature of such training courses since trainers and sometimes outside assessors need to have evidence that trainees have acquired the classroom skills specified in the course programme, but, as Maingay mentions, observation for assessment purposes also takes place when there is an inspection or audit by an external body. In Chapter 5, we also considered observation as a tool for assessing development (and perhaps training) needs. Maingay would probably include this as part of observation for development. This is the kind of observation that is likely to take place most often within a language teaching institution. Maingay suggests that, in feedback on such observation, 'an observer will be leading the observed teacher towards self-appraisal (including looking afresh at behaviour that may have become ritual) and towards developing new ideas for him or herself' (1988, p. 121).

The actual purposes of lesson observations in an institution may not be made clear to teachers (or observers), and thus the objectives of a given observation are not always communicated to the observed teacher. This may be because any lesson observation can combine different aims on the part of the observer: for example, checking the quality and effectiveness of teaching may be one of the aims, especially when an external inspection or audit is being prepared for, but in the feedback the focus may be on asking the observed teacher questions to promote self-awareness, and offering advice and pointers for future development. Furthermore, some observations may have a declared or undeclared focus on specific aspects or techniques of teaching, often specified in a checklist. Alternatively, the observation may be general and subjective, in which case observers may simply note down approximately what happened and record their views on what worked well (i.e. what they considered good) and what did not (what they considered not so good).

In summary, there is nothing wrong with having more than one objective in mind when carrying out lesson observation. Indeed, it may be hard to prevent oneself from assessing the quality of teaching, and of the support given to learning, while also aiming to work with the teacher on the principles behind 'ritual behaviour', and on identifying development needs. It is, however, important that the main aim of an observation is in the end achieved, and that the observed teacher gains something from the experience.

Observation for assessing development needs

In Chapter 5, observation was mentioned as one source of evidence to facilitate at least a partial assessment of the observed teacher's development needs. As with observations for other purposes, a key point that both the teacher being observed and the observer need to bear in mind is that the attention of the observer is as much focused on the students, and what and how they are learning, as on the teacher and how they are guiding and supporting that learning. Both are important in determining professional development needs.

In Bailey's (2006) terms, such observations are likely to be announced or negotiated, and possibly invited (or even unseen), especially where the teacher in question is concerned about a specific problem area. Other common characteristics are summarized in Figure 6.3.

Having an assessment objective during observation should not mean that the observer is searching for weaknesses or limitations in a teacher's performance. That would imply a deficit view of the teachers being observed – a focus on what they can't do rather on what they can do, or rather, the extent to which they can do things well. The emphasis should instead be on areas where small- or larger-scale development of awareness and skills would make a big difference from the students' point of view.

Who is the observer?	LCM, mentor, or trainer
Meeting or conversation beforehand?	Yes, if possible
Plan given to the observer beforehand?	Yes
Frequency of observation?	Ideally in a series
Length of observation?	Whole lesson, unless agreed otherwise
Recording during the observation?	Can be useful
Specific criteria or focus points?	If there is an agreed focus
Feedback discussion – how soon?	Very important – as soon as possible
Written record of the observation and feedback?	Yes, and should be agreed, especially development priorities and steps

Figure 6.3 Common characteristics of observation to assess a teacher's development needs

Activity 6.3 Imagine that you are planning to observe teachers in your institution with a view to helping them to identify some development needs. You decide to draw up a list of questions for yourself as an observer that can also be shared with the observed teacher. What questions would you include in your list?

The key questions for the observer in Activity 6.3 are likely to include the following:

- What are the teacher's aims in this lesson? (The plan for the lesson should be looked at and preferably discussed with the teacher beforehand.)
- Do the planned activities and actions in the lesson fit well with the aims?
- Do the students know what their learning aims are, and do they understand how the activities they are asked to engage in help them towards these learning aims?
- Is the plan being followed during the lesson? If not, why not?
- Are the planned and unplanned activities/events appropriate to the aims and for learners' needs?
- What is the teacher I am observing good at? Are the following having a positive, neutral, or negative impact on students' motivation and learning, and why?
    - the pace or length of activities
    - the way instructions and explanations are given

- the teacher's voice and body language
- the way the teacher handles student responses and errors
- the topic and materials selected
- other aspects

- In my opinion as an observer, could the given activity have been carried out more effectively from the point of view of students? If so, what could have been done differently?
- On the basis of the evidence, are there areas where the teacher could develop further their competence as a teacher? If so, how could that be done, and how could the institution and/or colleagues support that development?

Such observations—indeed, most observations—require time to be set aside for discussion or feedback afterwards. Given that teacher development is mainly the responsibility of the teacher concerned, it is not for the observer alone to decide on teachers' development needs. It makes sense to start from where teachers are or see themselves as being.

Activity 6.4

Irena is an LCM at a language school in Prague. She has just observed Markus teaching German to a low-level group of teenagers. Markus's teaching style is lively and he has a good relationship with the class. However, Irena has found that on more than one occasion a lot of time is spent on 'fun activities' that don't seem to have much potential for language learning, and the students don't seem to know what the purpose of these activities is (apart from enjoyment). She definitely doesn't want to demotivate Markus, but rather to get him thinking about other ways of teaching these teenagers.

If you were advising Irena on her approach to feedback in this case, what would your main advice be?

It is worth considering whether conversations between observers and observed teachers should be called 'feedback'. The term implies that the main purpose of any such discussion is for observers to tell teachers what they think about the teaching they have observed. In fact, in most cases it is more important to first get teachers themselves to recollect and reflect on what happened in the teaching, especially on what went well from their point of view, and what they felt went less well. In this case, Irena needs to allow Markus to highlight the parts of the lesson he is pleased with and the positive responses from the students, and she may be able to agree with him on this and offer praise. But she also needs to have some questions prepared that challenge Markus's own views and get him to think about the balance of fun activities and more serious language development and practice activities. She could, for example, point out that the fun activities will be that much more appreciated if they are balanced with activities that stretch students and require even the stronger students to make an effort. She may also be able to point to the fact that students actually practised or learned relatively little language in the time available, even though they had a good time.

In a way, the most important part of most observation events is the discussion afterwards. It is during this review of what went on in the lesson that the observed teacher and the observer can reflect together on where further development of skills and awareness could be beneficial. In an ideal situation, a dialogue in the form of genuine questions from the observer and thoughtful responses from the observed teacher can lead to agreement both about the strengths of the teaching observed and about areas where development or change is desirable.

If a recording of the lesson or parts of it is available for the teacher and the observer to view together and to comment on, the discussion is likely to be richer and the development priorities may be easier to agree. But in any case, there also needs to be sufficient time to agree the steps or actions that could be taken before the observation is followed up.

Self-recording and self-observation by teachers is still relatively uncommon, although it has become technically much easier to organize thanks to mobile devices with cameras and lower cost video and audio recording equipment. The factor in teaching institutions that may most limit how much recording of lessons and reviewing of the recording actually takes place is whether the promotion and development of a culture of openness to self-assessment and reflection has been successful. As discussed in Chapters 4 and 5, such a culture and the willingness to work in close collaboration with colleagues are essential if the quality and effectiveness of teaching are really to be improved over time.

Observation for supporting professional development

Observations that aim to support a teacher's development, which should preferably be negotiated or invited, generally assume that development needs have already been identified and agreed. Often, observations of this kind follow up development steps that were previously agreed in order to see how the teacher is applying the skills developed in practice and to offer further support if needed. Again, the observer will be focusing on students' learning as well as on how the teacher facilitates that learning. Some common characteristics of such observations are listed in Figure 6.4.

Who is the observer?	LCM, mentor, or trainer
Meeting or conversation beforehand?	Yes, definitely
Plan given to the observer beforehand?	Yes
Frequency of observation?	Ideally part of a series
Length of observation?	Could be section(s) of the lesson agreed with the teacher
Recording during the observation?	Can be very useful
Specific criteria or focus points?	Yes, focus on previously agreed development aims
Feedback discussion – how soon?	Very important – as soon as possible
Written record of the observation and feedback?	Yes, and should be agreed, especially further steps and follow-up

Figure 6.4 Common characteristics of observation to support teacher development

Where new and less experienced teachers are concerned, the discussion of this kind of observation may take the form of training or coaching. In other words, the discussion may be more one-sided and the suggestions firmer than with more experienced teachers. More will be said about this kind of observation in Chapter 7, but the important point is that observation for development purposes generally forms part of a series of events or actions that contribute to a teacher's development, or the development of a group of teachers.

Activity 6.5 A group of three teachers have been working with a senior teacher on developing their knowledge and skills in the area of pronunciation teaching. The particular focus has been on helping students at elementary level to learn the sounds and word and sentence stress patterns of the target language. The group have read and discussed two articles about the subject and have worked with the senior teacher on adding pronunciation practice activities to their lesson plans. They have also attended a workshop on specific techniques for dealing with and giving feedback about pronunciation, and have watched a video of the senior teacher working with her own students. The senior teacher is now going to observe each of the three teachers. How should she prepare for and plan the observations, and what advice could you offer on handling the discussions after the observations?

In a way, this kind of 'developmental' observation is straightforward. The observer's focus is likely to be on the specific techniques that have been discussed and rehearsed with the teachers, such as demonstrative modelling of pronunciation and guided repetition, and the use of relevant resources, such as audio recordings, symbols, and underlining on the board or phonemic charts. This doesn't mean that other aspects of the teaching should be disregarded, but discussion of these afterwards will probably be separate from the discussion of the teaching of pronunciation. It is also unlikely that all three teachers will handle the techniques and resources in an identical way as they will have different personalities, and their students will react differently. Ideally, the observer wants to see and comment on the ways in which the teachers have shaped and exploited the techniques according to their individual needs and preferences. In other words, the observer will not be looking for uniformity or a right way of doing things, but will discuss with each teacher how their actions actually helped students with their pronunciation. Needless to say, being able to talk about video recordings of the relevant parts of these lessons would be very helpful in the post-observation discussion because concrete details that make a big difference to students' learning and motivation can be highlighted and talked about more easily.

As implied by Maingay (1988), observations for the purposes of development can be reversed so that the aim is for the observer rather than the observed teacher to learn from the experience. In the case of Activity 6.5, the three teachers did have an opportunity to view videos of the senior teacher 'demonstrating' techniques for teaching pronunciation. Arguably, they would also have learned a lot from watching each other but, regrettably, teachers seldom have time to observe lessons given by other teachers, due to busy timetables. As will be pointed out in Chapter 8, the value of peer observation and team-teaching as aids to development should not be underestimated.

Observations for quality assurance

Such observations, whether carried out by the LCM or by an external body, imply that standards exist which the institution aspires to or that the external body sets. Indeed, one reason why institutions seek inspection by external bodies is to advertise high standards that are linked to external points of reference and are used by all institutions who agree to undergo inspection or audit. As an example, Figure 6.5 lists the standards for 'Teaching and learning' from the Eaquals Quality Standards.

> 1 The pedagogical approach and methods reflect the institution's educational philosophy.
> 2 The quality of course delivery consistently provides opportunities for effective learning.
> 3 Lessons are planned with reference to the course programme and the learning and motivational needs of individuals and the group; specified learning outcomes are shared with learners.
> 4 The opportunities offered for learning are varied, making use of available technology and resources.
> 5 Learners have the opportunity to develop their study skills and to share responsibility for their own learning.

Figure 6.5 Standards for 'Teaching and learning' (Eaquals Quality Standards, see Website references)

These standards are accompanied by 'indicators of compliance with quality standards', as shown in Figure 6.6.

> - Coherence between the institution's stated educational philosophy and pedagogic approach (as set out in the relevant documents) and classroom practice is apparent.
> - Teaching quality is high, and clear learning opportunities for all learners are apparent in the classroom.
> - Evidence of principled planning and organization is to be found in lesson plans and other planning documents produced by teachers such as weekly plans and/or schemes of work. These reflect the institution's educational philosophy and pedagogical approach and are clearly based on course learning programmes.
> - Lesson plans, weekly plans, schemes of work, etc. include clear intended learning outcomes, and are shared in an appropriate way with learners, for example by display of relevant documents on notice boards and/or on the board, and by directing learners' attention as progress is made.
> - The content of the lessons, the materials used, and the methodology employed are suitable for the age, level and needs of the learners, and appropriate in the context of the course profile.
> - There is evidence of effective correction and teaching of pronunciation and intonation as appropriate for the learners (age, level, etc.) and the course objectives.

Figure 6.6 Indicators of compliance with quality standards (Eaquals, 2016a, p. 10)

Such quality assurance observations are frequently surprise ones, or, if announced, the actual time of the observation is not specified. Figure 6.7 lists some common characteristics of such observations.

Who is the observer?	LCM or external agency
Meeting or conversation beforehand?	No
Plan given to the observer beforehand?	No, but often requested in the classroom
Frequency of observation?	Can be one of a series where several teachers are observed in a day
Length of observation?	May be a whole lesson or only 15–20 minutes
Recording during the observation?	No
Specific criteria or focus points?	Yes, depending on the standards used
Feedback discussion – how soon?	Usually no individual feedback unless combined with development; general feedback on all observations provided to management
Written record of the observation and feedback?	Notes are normally made, but may not be shared directly with the teacher

Figure 6.7 Common characteristics of observations for quality assurance purposes

In this kind of observation, where the quality of teaching in general is being scrutinized and its compliance with the specified standards is being verified, there may be no direct feedback to individual teachers. Instead a general overview report may be produced identifying certain recommendations, and possibly areas where the standards are not met and work has to be done. Or if the quality assurance observations are run internally, for example on an annual basis, the LCM may give a general oral report to teachers highlighting areas of strength and areas where standards are not always met and further work is needed.

Another reason why observations with a quality assurance focus are carried out is to respond to feedback or complaints from students. In such cases, a clear focus is often implied by the feedback or complaint itself. Needless to say, the handling of the observation and especially the discussion afterwards needs to be very carefully thought through. Managing complaints from students about teachers' work in the classroom, which are generally rather uncommon, or about other aspects of teachers' behaviour, will be considered in Chapter 7.

Some guidelines on setting up and running observation schemes

Not all teachers are happy to be observed. Often, instead of seeing observations as useful and beneficial, they resent them or feel they are unproductive. Many teachers feel insecure about being observed: they are worried, no matter how much the value of observation is explained, that they are being judged professionally. For these teachers, rather than a positive experience, it becomes a stressful ordeal. This is a great pity because, used well and sensitively, observations can add greatly to teacher development and ultimately teacher effectiveness. Figure 6.8 offers some brief guidelines for LCMs on setting up or reviewing observation procedures within an institution.

Activity 6.6 What advice would you offer to someone in a new LCM or mentoring role who is about to observe teachers for the first time? Read through the section below and note down which three of the guidelines offered is most important according to your own experience.

Lesson plans and pre-observation discussion

It is advisable for observers to have a clear idea of what teachers are intending to do. How detailed the plan needs to be is an important decision: there is no point in teachers doing extra work on written plans if it isn't really needed. But even in quality assurance observations, the observer needs to have a plan available.

Do:	Don't:
• review practical options carefully, especially procedures that have been used before • think through the key issues and options discussed in this chapter • explain carefully why observations are necessary, and how they can help individuals, the team, and the organization; allow discussion of and questions about this • outline clearly the proposed scheme (or more than one alternative), using graphics such as a flow chart, explaining what happens at each step, and referring to differences as compared to any existing scheme or procedure that teachers may be familiar with • consider getting longer term teachers involved in the meeting and discussion so that they can comment on previous systems • allow questions and comments on this. If reasonable suggestions for changing it are made and supported by at least some of the team, make changes	• innovate for the sake of being different • stick with what you know, or miss out any important questions or points for discussion • assume that people will immediately understand your own and the employer's view of observations • simply say that teachers' lessons will be observed between dates X and Y, with no explanation of the detail • ignore the experience and opinions of teachers who have already formed views of what works well and doesn't work so well • close down or put obstacles (such as lack of time) in the way of a shared approach

Figure 6.8 'Dos and don'ts' when setting up or reviewing an observation system

A short discussion before the observation is valuable in most circumstances and can reduce the need for lengthy written plans. It provides an opportunity for teachers to talk about a range of relevant topics: the students, particularly differences in level, motivation, etc.; where they are in the syllabus or course programme; the resources they are using and their opinion of these; any areas of their teaching that they would like the observer to focus on; any difficulties they may be predicting. The preliminary discussion also enables the observer to clarify details about timing, focus (if any), follow-up discussion, and so on, and above all to try to reduce any stress that the teacher may be experiencing, which is more likely to be the case if teachers are not used to being observed or have had unhappy experiences with it. It is also an opportunity to go through the observation record form and criteria being used with the teacher.

Recording or not?

The best way of recording will depend on the classroom size and layout as well as the equipment available. It makes sense for institutions to invest in a small video camera, a tripod, and additional microphones—especially a wireless lapel microphone for the teacher—if needed. The camera on a tripod can be placed in a position such that most of what the teacher does is recorded. If it can also record clearly some of the students' responses (for example one side of the room), so much the better.

However, the decision as to whether recording can take place, and for how long and of which parts of the lesson, should rest with the teacher. It is often best if teachers first have experience of recording themselves, even if just for a few minutes, and observing and commenting on the recording to overcome the likely shock of such self-observation. Written permission also needs to be obtained from the students, even if the recording is only going to be viewed privately.

One of the aims is that both the students and the teacher eventually stop noticing that recording is taking place.

During the observation

What is known as the 'observer's paradox', i.e. that the presence of the observer itself affects what happens in the event being observed (Labov, 1972), is a factor to be aware of. What any observer hopes for is teaching and learning that is as close as possible to what normally takes place. The observer needs to be as unobtrusive as possible and not at all a focus of attention. So, choosing the right place to sit and avoiding active involvement are important.

Note-taking is important, even when recording is taking place, but it needs to provide the necessary reference points for later discussion. Some institutions and managers have different observation sheets and checklists for different purposes. The method used will depend on the individual LCM and the purposes of observation. If a checklist is used or specific focus points are listed to facilitate note-taking, it is essential to inform teachers what these are.

After the observation – no recording

If the observer stays to the end of the lesson, it is good to say something positive and to confirm arrangements for the later discussion immediately. The meeting should take place as soon as possible, especially if there has been no recording, in order to ensure that important aspects are not forgotten, and also to avoid stress on the part of the teacher.

Whatever the purpose of observation, but especially if an objective is to agree some development needs and objectives or to aid development, it is important that sufficient time is allowed for the discussion, that it takes place in a quiet environment, and that it is confidential.

A good way of beginning is to ask the observed teacher how they thought the lesson went in general, and what their feelings were after the lesson. We all experience some kind of sensation after teaching – frustration, relief, satisfaction, excitement. Whatever the overall feeling, it opens up a series of questions about why the teacher did things in a certain way, what was most/least satisfying, what part of the lesson went best, etc.

A next step is to go through the plan and/or the actual steps as recorded in the notes, to remind both the observer and the teacher what actually happened. This exercise enables the teacher to remember and reflect and the observer to ask further questions, such as:

- Why did you … ?
- Can you think of any other way of doing that?
- Why do you think student X reacted in that way?
- Were you happy with … ?

The aim is to methodically gather the teacher's own views and reflections on what happened. However, each of the answers may open the way for follow-up suggestions from the observer. Some observers prefer to do this in a more tentative way:

- Do you think it might have been better to … ?
- Could you maybe have spent a little longer … ?

Others will take a more direct approach, especially with less experienced teachers:

- I think it would have been better to …
- I felt that you didn't allow students enough time to …

There are two other important points. First, it is not necessary and probably not desirable to be exhaustive, in other words to go over every minute of the lesson. It is more relevant to pick out examples of really good teaching, and some others where an alternative course of action would have worked better. This is especially important where the focus is on specific areas that the teacher has worked on. The aim is definitely to encourage the teacher, so it is important to identify strong points as well as to focus on a few areas where the teacher can agree that a different approach would have been better or can see options for further development. Second, the meeting needs to end with a summary both of the strong points and the points that both the observer and the teacher agree need to be worked on, and if possible an indication of how and when they will be worked on.

After the observation – with recording

Broadly, the process can be the same. However, now the observer and teacher can watch parts of the lesson together. They need to agree how the clips they will watch together will be selected, and whether they can both pause the recording when they wish to – in the case of the teacher, to make a comment or ask for advice, and in the case of the observer, to ask questions and make suggestions.

A big advantage is that the clip can be watched more than once and details can be properly discussed. Looking at the 'evidence' in this way makes it easier to ask questions about and discuss details such as the language used, the teacher's voice and body language, the reactions of students and the general effectiveness of each activity (or even each interaction); and this discussion can lead to general points about possible changes or further improvements, and how the teacher can move towards making them. Good examples of this kind of discussion in a mainstream school environment can be found in videos on the Teachers Media International website (see Website references).

Consistency

Once a set of observation procedures is understood and agreed to, it is important for members of staff to feel that it is applied consistently and will not suddenly and without warning be changed. For example, if teachers agree to video-record sections of certain lessons, then review the video, and then discuss it with their LCM who did not observe the lesson, it might be off-putting if the LCM suddenly decides to observe the next lesson live without first explaining why and allowing for discussion.

Equally, staff members like to feel that, if the group have agreed to a certain system, it will be applied in a similar way to all and not that some teachers' lessons will be observed much less frequently or in a different way.

Having opportunities to comment on procedures in regular reviews and seeing them change in small ways as a result of feedback inspires confidence in the continuation of a team approach.

Conclusion

This chapter has explored lesson observation in some detail as a management tool and a means of teacher development. It has been stressed that, while observation can have a positive impact on teachers' professional development and on quality in the classroom, the procedures and arrangements for lesson observation of different kinds need to be very carefully thought through and discussed with the teachers who are going to be observed. The aim, after all, is that teachers, students, and the institution should benefit from the outcomes of such observations, certainly not that teachers should be fearful of or threatened by them.

The observers who have not been mentioned but do more observation than anyone else are the students. It is seldom that teachers discuss with students their opinions and feedback on the teaching that they 'observe' and the learning that they participate in. It could be argued that important opportunities are missed if students are not consulted and that, potentially, their feedback and views are as important as those of the managers, who observe lessons much less regularly. The subject of student feedback and how to obtain and use it will be considered in Chapter 8.

PART THREE

7 PERFORMANCE MANAGEMENT

Introduction

Chapters 4, 5, and 6 have been concerned primarily with teachers' professional development. Another important and related aspect of managing employees, including teachers, is reviewing how they perform their role in the institution. Performance reviews happen in different ways, in different contexts and cultures: in some contexts, it is done in a casual, intermittent way, with the LCM asking questions such as 'How are you getting on with group X?', 'How is project Y going?', and perhaps giving gentle reminders such as 'Have you managed to do that report I asked for?', 'Why haven't you filled in the class record?'. In other environments and institutions, there is a more formal system with planned and detailed individual meetings at least once a year and other intermittent contacts to check progress, with ongoing records of these encounters. However it is done, overseeing the work and performance of teachers (and sometimes other employees) is an integral part of the LCM's role. If there is no kind of performance management, there is a danger that teachers and other staff simply don't feel acknowledged, don't know how well they are doing their job, and don't know whether their work is considered good or average. This can be damaging for morale and may lead to a feeling that people can do what they like, however they like, which can undermine the team approach and sense of collective purpose necessary for a well-functioning, high-quality organization. This chapter will consider fairly methodical approaches to the task of managing the performance of teachers and other staff, whilst recognizing that styles and methods vary considerably depending on national and institutional cultures.

The rather forbidding term 'performance management' covers the roles in management that concern the quality and impact of employees' work and general contribution to their organization. Parts of this role can be performed informally through everyday interactions with colleagues in which they are asked about how their work is going, what is causing them concern or giving them satisfaction, and requests for or offers of advice and guidance. Performance management also includes the more formal activity of performance appraisal ('appraisal' for short). That is, the regular evaluation and discussion in individual meetings of how well individual employees are performing, a process that causes some employees—and certain managers—alarm and disenchantment. On the other hand, performance management also encompasses aspects of professional development that were discussed in Chapter 5, and this is often reviewed and planned in appraisal meetings.

The Chartered Institute of Personnel and Development (CIPD) in the UK defines performance management at its best as a holistic process that ensures employees' performance contributes to business objectives. It brings together many elements of good people management practice, including learning and development, measurement of performance, and organizational development (see Website references). The phrase 'at its best' highlights a key issue with performance management, namely that it can be—and often is—badly handled.

When discussing performance management in the context of language education, which they state is 'central to human resources management and indeed management in general', White et al. (2008) ask 'how can you manage, monitor, and evaluate [employees'] performance in a non-intrusive way that does not demotivate?' (p. 65). Managers in educational institutions, especially those in the public sector, may consider that the reference to business objectives in the CIPD definition referred to above reduces the relevance of performance management for them. We can, however, easily substitute 'business objectives' with 'institutional objectives' or 'mission'.

Appraisal

Activity 7.1 Have you ever participated in an appraisal meeting as a manager or employee? If so, what do you remember about the situation and the outcomes? What was positive about it, and were there any negative aspects?

A common problem with appraisal is that it is often not clear exactly what functions it serves, and it is not easy to run a system that serves vague or multiple purposes. Traditionally, appraisal has often been associated with remuneration and pay progression. When appraisal became part of human resources management in the mid 20th century, its main purpose was to relate performance—in terms of work rate, initiative, sales, etc.—over the past year to future pay or bonuses, in other words, to offer incentives to employees doing well, and potentially to penalize those who were not. It also has to be remembered that the concept of appraisal has specific cultural overtones having originally been developed in the context of US and northern European working practices, where a key aim was incentivization and steady improvement, especially in terms of productivity or results. This approach is still common among, for example, investment bankers, who may receive large bonuses related to the success of their investment work. But, as the last sentence of the CIPD factsheet 'What is performance management?' emphasizes, for performance management to be successfully introduced and serve its purpose, employees and their managers must be able to have open and meaningful discussions of objectives and professional development needs, which are related to the strategy and objectives of the organization, rather than possible pay increases related to their performance.

Where appraisals in the context of human resources management generally are concerned, Lewthwaite (2006) identifies the following possible purposes: evaluation of performance, audit of work potential, training **needs analysis**, motivation, development, planning, and control. As she says, 'seven sets of objectives, some of which overlap, and some of which may contradict, are unlikely to lead to clear processes within the appraisal interview' (pp. 208–209). Lewthwaite goes on to distil these multiple objectives into three main areas of focus: development, performance, and reward.

It may well be found that, in certain contexts, attitudes to appraisal and related practices are unfavourable because they do not fit in with national or sectoral working practices, especially where educational institutions are concerned. In spite of globalization, workplace and human resources practices vary considerably according to national cultural traditions, so approaches to performance management must be designed to fit in with the cultural context and 'what works best' in a given employment situation. For example, if employees feel in any way threatened by the process of appraisal, they are unlikely to see it in a positive light. But that doesn't mean that there is no place for performance management or that employees cannot come to see the advantages to them of participating in appraisals: periodic reviews and discussions with individuals can provide excellent opportunities for constructive exchange between individual employees and their manager, and can lead to better working relationships and opportunities for professional development.

Purposes, approaches, and systems of performance management

Activity 7.2

You are a recently appointed LCM at a medium-sized institution in the UK. There are 20 teachers, some of them part-time, teaching English mainly to young adults from around the world preparing to study at university level in the medium of English. Over the past few years, there has been no organized performance management system in the institution, but you believe it is necessary, especially as you do not know the teachers well.

In designing the system, what would you want to get out of it, and what elements would you want to include? How would you explain the purposes and functioning of the system to teachers?

As mentioned above, the main point of the appraisal procedure is that it is, among other things, an opportunity for employees, in this case teachers, to sit down with their LCM to review their relationship and role, especially in terms of how they have contributed and are contributing to the aims and work of the institution, and how the institution has supported them in their work as well as their professional and career development. As was seen in Chapter 4, identifying and agreeing development needs with teachers is a crucial element of performance management, since it is mainly through professional development that individual performance can improve over time. Also, it is essential for managers to quickly identify serious problems with performance or with conduct, such as routine lateness, bullying of colleagues, etc. which might not be visible in observations or in students' feedback. Other purposes of performance management may include the following elements:

- Incentivization: a key objective, possibly in the sense of improved career prospects and remuneration discussed earlier in the chapter, but more commonly in the sense of encouraging and motivating teachers by indicating how maintaining high standards of 'performance' and dealing well with new challenges can lead to new opportunities, if not to higher pay or a bonus.
- Future planning: knowing what a teacher is capable of both in the classroom and outside is important, but in order to decide who should be assigned to what teaching and other duties in the next period it is also essential to know about teachers' intentions (e.g. will they still be available for work at the same times?) and preferences (e.g. they are good at teaching students planning to study science, but are they willing to continue doing that, or do they want a change?). Related to this is 'lack of appetite' for—or a lack of confidence in—some of the teaching they have been doing: teachers who feel unhappy about teaching certain kinds of classes are unlikely to perform well if given similar classes next time, unless they are helped and can rebuild their confidence and competence.
- Feedback: performance management can provide good opportunities to give teachers feedback not just on their teaching of a specific class, as happens after an observation, but about their work in general across all their teaching, including their work outside the classroom (materials development, extracurricular activities with students, test invigilation and marking, etc.). Equally importantly, it provides opportunities for obtaining feedback on all aspects of the institution, including the LCMs' ways of working with teachers.

Another purpose—and advantage—of appraisal meetings is that they enable LCMs, especially when newly appointed, to get to know and understand teachers better at an individual level. It is hard for any LCM to spend significant time with each teacher in the busy daily functioning of an institution, especially if some of them are part-time, and it is not uncommon for teachers' performance and well-being to be affected by issues in their daily lives.

As noted above, a common problem with performance management is that it can be focused excessively on the appraisal meeting, which is usually only once a year, and its aftermath. In fact, it should be conceived of as an ongoing process and an integral part of team management year-round, and needs to be linked with tracking and supporting professional development, gathering feedback from students, and institutional development. As with lesson observation (see Chapter 6), it is important for teachers to fully understand the purposes of the performance management system and how it will work, and to have opportunities to ask questions about it and make suggestions. With this in mind, the LCM in Activity 7.2 might envisage a four-stage cycle like the one shown in Figure 7.1.

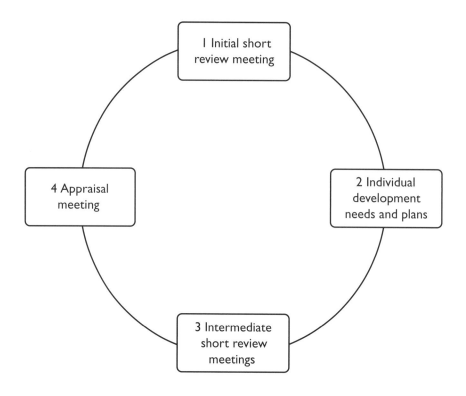

Figure 7.1 Suggested four-stage cycle for performance management

A new performance management system and its aims need to be documented clearly and discussed and agreed with teachers. The system also needs reviewing after a period to check that it is working as was hoped, and to make adjustments if not. Once the system is established it needs to be explained to new members of staff as part of the induction process (see Chapter 3).

1 Initial short review meeting

Activity 7.3 You have decided to adopt the performance management cycle as outlined in Figure 7.1. What main points do you want to address in the initial short review meeting?

The purpose of the initial short review meeting is for the LCM to get to know new members of the teaching staff, to find out more about or deepen one's acquaintance with teachers that the LCM doesn't know well, or to obtain a brief update with well-established team members. In institutions with year-long courses such as mainstream schools and colleges, or language institutes offering part-time courses to the local community, this could easily be combined with the meeting at which the LCM assigns to each teacher the classes to be taught in the coming period. For logistical reasons it may be that the classes have been assigned to teachers via a timetable or individual emails, but where the teaching team is not too large—say, fewer than 20 people—it is good policy to arrange a short meeting with each teacher in order to go through the classes assigned and deal with any questions. If there are also coordinators or assistant managers/supervisors, the meetings with members of a large team can be divided among them. This initial meeting not only increases the human contact between LCMs and individual teachers: it also allows for discussion of other issues, including concerns teachers may have about their work.

In institutions such as private language schools and colleges offering intensive and often very short courses in the language of the country to students from abroad, the discussion may be less specific because teachers' duties may change frequently, and indeed teachers on short-term or flexible contracts may not even have guaranteed work for more than a week or two at a time. Such situations actually make personal contact with the LCM more important. Figure 7.2 suggests objectives and topics for these initial short review meetings at the beginning of the semester or course period.

New teachers and those the LCM does not know well	Established teachers the LCM knows well
• Seek information (or more information) about the teacher's past experience, training, personal situation, and own views and interests. • Get feedback on induction process and/or first few weeks. • Go through classes proposed for teacher's timetable, dealing with questions and concerns; be prepared to make changes if serious concerns arise. • Explain about planned observations, how professional development needs will be assessed, etc. and answer questions about this.	• Reconnect with them and get an update on their circumstances and the course(s) they have taught since the last conversation. • Identify any ongoing or new concerns the teacher may have about their work. • Go through classes (and possible other duties) proposed for the teacher's timetable, linking these to the teacher's past work; deal with any questions or concerns. • Discuss proposed approach to individual professional development, especially the teacher's own ideas and special interests, and agree observation plans.
Additional – for short-course centres	
• Explain how assigning teachers to courses is handled. • Deal with questions about how far in advance teachers will know their timetable for the next week(s) and what happens when work is not available.	• Explain general approach to assignment of courses to such teachers. • Deal with special requests and concerns.

Figure 7.2 Suggested objectives for initial short review meetings

It has to be borne in mind that these meetings need to be kept short—no more than 10 minutes (15 minutes with newer teachers)—so as not to take too much time away from the LCM. For example, this will take several hours with a team of 20 or more. While the meetings could be divided among two or three different

LCMs coordinating different levels, there is the disadvantage that an overview of the whole team cannot so easily be gained. There may also be no easy opportunity to schedule such meetings unless teachers are willing to come in on a relevant day before the course period starts. It may, however, be possible to arrange a phone conversation which many teachers and LCMs will find more satisfactory than email. As mentioned in Chapter 5, some institutions run short conferences at the beginning of the teaching period to facilitate a special focus on professional development topics. These events can provide a good opportunity for arranging such individual meetings, although the LCM would then be unable to participate in the group activities for a lengthy period. Either way, it is important to timetable the meetings, indicating specific times and likely duration, providing a brief outline of the objectives, and asking whether the teacher wishes to discuss any other topics ahead of time.

It is clear that such meetings are generally well worth the time involved: they provide an opportunity for one-to-one contact which is usually much appreciated, and enable the LCM to remind themselves about their team as individuals as well as to discuss each teacher's work for the next period.

2 Individual development needs and plans

As discussed in Chapter 5, professional development both at individual and team level is ongoing. The first meetings with individuals provide an opportunity for the LCM to review 'progress so far' and plans for the next period. This is much easier if each teacher has a teacher's log. In parallel, at a meeting with the whole team, plans for group development activities can be put in place or confirmed.

3 Intermediate short review meetings

One or more shorter catch-up meetings with the LCM enable the teacher to talk about current teaching duties, especially any difficulties, and to give an update on progress with professional development. The objective for the LCM is to react to the teacher's concerns about current work or other issues, and to obtain information about individual professional development steps and activities so far and how the teacher feels about progress, especially its impact on teaching. The meetings also provide opportunities for the LCM to give encouragement, offer advice or make further suggestions, sort out misunderstandings, and so on.

The meetings themselves, like lesson observations, are only part of the process. Any planned meeting, unlike the more casual encounters that happen daily, needs preparation by both parties, especially the LCM. For example, what aspects of performance in general and teaching in particular are worthy of comment? What questions can be asked about progress with professional development? Is there any particular issue that needs to be discussed or brought to the teacher's attention?

Afterwards, notes on each meeting need to be agreed between the LCM and teacher and added to the records kept by both. Teachers also have the opportunity of commenting individually on the process and its outcomes in their teacher's log if they have one. A way of handling this in the context of a busy educational institution is to use forms or templates developed for the purpose, with a standard list of questions which can be added to in a flexible way when there is a need.

4 Appraisal meetings

Activity 7.4 If the system also includes a longer, more wide-ranging appraisal meeting towards the end of the academic year or course period, what would its main objectives be? As an LCM, how would you ask teachers to prepare for it?

In an educational environment there are four main areas that are useful to cover with teachers (and other staff) in such longer annual individual meetings which, if handled well, can be very beneficial for all concerned:

- a review of performance and achievements over the period: from both the teacher's view and the LCM's view
- individual professional development: again, progress from the teacher's point of view and the institution's
- feedback to the LCM on the systems used in the institution and developments taking place, as well as on the way the LCM has managed the individual and the team
- a look forward to plans and objectives for the next period: institutional priorities relevant to the teacher, and the teacher's own plans and objectives.

Where these longer appraisal meetings are concerned, preparation is doubly important and questionnaires that can be filled in electronically, returned to the LCM, and later annotated have proved to be a good means of stimulating preparation both by the teacher and by the LCM. A sample questionnaire that can be easily adapted is offered in Appendix 2 (see page 173). The list of points to cover in this questionnaire is quite long, though of course it would need adapting to the specific context, and could be divided up between more than one meeting. In all cases, it is essential that teachers complete the questionnaire before the meeting, even if they only put brief notes in response to some items. If the potential advantages of appraisal meetings have been made clear to teachers, each individual should regard their meeting as a good opportunity to 'make their voice heard', and preparation can only help them to do that. It is important also for the LCM to emphasize that what is said in the meeting will be taken seriously and, for relevant items, will remain confidential. What is expected is that teachers will speak honestly and frankly, and so the LCM's responses need to be measured and accompanied by follow-up questions where necessary. It may happen that the teacher becomes emotional, depending on the strength of his or her opinions, and on the nature of the feedback they hear from the manager. This brings us back to Heron's six categories of interaction (2001; see page 49): the balance between facilitative interaction and authoritative interaction needs to be carefully maintained in such situations, and the meeting must end in some kind of agreement. In rare cases, it may be necessary to adjourn the meeting and continue it at a later time (preferably not a later date).

Disciplinary matters and grievances

A good performance management system and positive ongoing relationships between the LCM and teachers can make a significant difference to the general climate in an institution, and to the quality and effectiveness of the work of all concerned. It is, however, important for the LCM to be prepared for performance problems or complaints that need immediate attention in order to avoid disrupting the positive climate and good work. 'Disciplinary matters' include all those instances of behaviour that potentially breach the rules specified in or implied by the employee's contract, while 'grievances' is the term used for instances where employees are seriously unhappy about the way in which they are treated by their employer or a member of the employer's staff.

Disciplinary matters

Activity 7.5

Consider scenario 1, below. What course of action do you think you should follow? What guidelines should your institution provide about handling such situations, and what should staff know about the process?

Scenario 1: One of the teachers in your institution is habitually late, especially on certain days of the week. This means the lesson begins late, or has to be substituted by you for a short period, and some of the students have complained. You have asked the teacher why he is late but not received a clear answer, just an apology and a promise that it won't happen again. But it has, several times.

As in other organizations, in educational institutions, employees (including managers) do not always follow internal rules conscientiously and they occasionally make mistakes or have lapses. While this has to be accepted as a 'fact of life', it is important for institutions to have in place an established system for dealing with substandard behaviour and performance. But before putting such a system in place, there needs to be a clear statement of the standards of behaviour expected. This can be in the form of a code of conduct which is appended to staff contracts and dealt with during the induction process. Apart from obvious general topics such as honesty, carrying out the responsibilities specified in the job description, avoiding discrimination of any kind, and not bringing the institution into disrepute, there may be specific rules about, for example, what to do when a member of staff has to be absent or cannot arrive in time. This is so that measures can be taken to deal with absence or lateness. There may also be rules about dress code (what to wear or what not to wear), relations with students (what kind of contact is and is not permitted), and the handling of non-teaching duties such as the marking of homework, attending meetings, and so on. Not having such a list of clear standards can make the implementation of disciplinary procedures, when there is a need to, much more difficult. In scenario 1 outlined in Activity 7.5, a common procedure is a series of warning stages such as the following:

1 First verbal warning, with a request such as 'please don't do it again' or 'please follow the procedure properly next time' (which, in scenario 1, the LCM has already completed).

2 Second verbal warning, expressed more strongly than the first. This could be followed up with a written record of the warning, including the date, the degree of lateness, and the nature of the warning (e.g. what the consequences will be if it happens again).

3 Final written warning in the form of a formal letter to the employee, making it clear that this is the third and final warning. The letter should specify the details and dates of the lapses in punctuality, and outline what consequences will follow on the next occasion (such as a formal disciplinary interview).

It needs to be stressed that this is just one possible process and that, depending on the context, such procedures may be specified in national labour law or in procedures formally agreed between the employer and employee representatives or their trade union(s). The main points are that there needs to be a procedure, that employees need to know what it is, and that the institution needs to follow it. Such procedures also generally include special steps for cases of 'gross misconduct', such as theft of institutional property, harassment and bullying, being under the influence of alcohol or other drugs while at work, and so on. Depending on national employment legislation, the special steps might include suspension, instant dismissal from work, and/or legal action. Such incidents may never have occurred in a given institution, but everyone needs to know what happens if they ever do occur.

Grievances

Activity 7.6

Consider scenario 2. What procedure do you think should be used for handling this grievance?

Scenario 2: Another teacher at your institution has recently complained verbally that she has been treated unfairly compared to other teachers. Her timetable is split every day except Friday between morning classes starting at 8am and evening classes between 5 and 9pm. Some other teachers, especially male teachers who have worked there for several years, only work 'split shifts' of this kind two days a week.

The other side of the disciplinary coin is grievances held—or complaints made—by employees about their employer's or a colleague's conduct or, for example, their conditions of work. As with discipline, such cases need to be handled sensitively and consistently according to a procedure known to members of staff and management. This may also be partly specified by national legislation or in their contracts of employment, but it still needs to be brought to the attention of all concerned. In the case of scenario 2 outlined in Activity 7.6, the procedure could, for example, involve the following steps:

1 The LCM requests that the grievance be put in writing so it is clearly recorded. This could be important at a later stage.

2 The LCM looks into the facts of the matter: how many teachers are on similar 'split shift' timetables? Why is this kind of timetable necessary, and was it specified in the teacher's original contract? Is it true that some or most long-standing staff do not have such contracts, and are they mainly male teachers? This last point could be important because of equal opportunities legislation in many countries.

3 Report findings back to the teacher. In reporting back, the LCM would go through the information with the teacher and, if necessary, concede that there is a problem which will be addressed as soon as it can be. If there is nothing unusual or objectively unfair about the situation (for example, because timetables change every three months and those teachers on split shifts will not have them next time around), the LCM will explain why the situation is as it is at the moment, and could perhaps offer to help lighten the teacher's load in some way by moving her from a difficult late or early class to an easier one.

4 Establish whether further action needs to be taken by asking the teacher whether her grievance can be considered resolved. If the grievance can be considered resolved, or if action is to be taken that will resolve it, this needs to be recorded in writing and signed by the teacher. If the teacher wishes to take it further, another more formal meeting will need to be planned, possibly with the Director of the institution, for which the written records of meetings so far will provide background.

Grievances that cannot be resolved in a single meeting with the LCM are thankfully not that common, and more serious grievances, for example about bullying between employees or breach of contract by the employer, are even rarer. It is, however, essential for institutions and their managers to be prepared for them so as to avoid time-consuming difficulties and stressful situations for all concerned.

Conclusion

This chapter has dealt with the sensitive matter of managing teachers' performance. This involves establishing simple and clear procedures that enable LCMs to keep in regular touch with individual teachers so that, on the one hand, they are aware of teachers' individual personalities and circumstances, as well as the quality of their work in and outside the classroom, and their professional development needs and their progress towards these; and on the other, that all teachers feel that their individual strengths and needs are taken into account, and know what is expected of them in terms of both performance and professional development. Generally, employees like to know where they stand, to be recognized for their achievements, and to be guided where necessary. Performance management is also concerned with the contribution that teachers are making to the institution's aims, but the expectation is that teachers and LCMs are all, in the end, focused on the best interests of the students and their progress. The purpose of performance management is to establish and maintain the open but structured positive team and individual relationships that encourage employees to work to high standards and to continue to grow professionally, and in the case of teachers, to ensure that students consistently receive high-quality and effective support for their language learning.

8 COURSE DESIGN, NEEDS ANALYSIS, AND ASSESSMENT OF LANGUAGE LEARNING

Introduction

This chapter focuses on another key area of the LCM's job in most centres: the course programme itself, the processes which shape the course objectives, the content and methodology of the course, and the way in which learning outcomes and students' progress are assessed. These are critical factors in the quality and effectiveness of the learning opportunities offered to students and, to a large extent, provide the framework for the work of language teachers.

Given the broad scope of this book, the exploration of the roles and tasks of LCMs in this area will be at a general level. The third title in the series, *Language Course Planning*, will explore the area of course design and assessment in much more detail.

Course Design

Activity 8.1

David, who has several years' experience as a teacher of English in three different countries and has worked as a coordinator at a school in Italy, has just been appointed as Director of Studies at a newly established language centre in Slovenia. The owners, who are not themselves specialists in languages, but are entrepreneurs who have carried out some market research, intend to offer courses in English to adults and children, as well as in Italian and German. They are especially keen to work with international companies whose employees need these languages for work purposes.

When he arrives, David is told that his first job is to design the courses that will start to run when the new academic year begins in two months' time. David is excited to be given so much responsibility, having previously worked in well-established centres, and is anxious to make sure things start well. What steps will he need to go through, and what systems and documents will he need to prepare?

One of the exciting aspects of working in independent language centres like the one in Activity 8.1 is that there may be much more freedom and flexibility in the way things are done because course fees are paid by students and by other customers who require courses for students. The challenge is, therefore, to find ways to respond well to the demands of the market so that plenty of students enrol. The process that David needs to go through is critical to the success of the new venture. Course design is one of twelve standards outlined in the Eaquals Quality Standards, the first of which states that there should be 'a statement of the institution's educational philosophy and written descriptions of its learning programmes, including course objectives and content' (Eaquals, see Website references). To guide the work of teachers at the new centre, David will need to create documentation that explains the institution's philosophy and approach to learning and outlines the course programmes.

Documentation: curriculum and syllabus

There is often confusion, at least in English, around the terms 'curriculum' and 'syllabus'. For our purposes, the term 'curriculum' denotes a document, or part of a document, that includes a brief outline of the institution's educational philosophy mentioned in the Eaquals Quality Standards above, as a prelude to providing an overview of its educational offer. That is, the curriculum provides a framework within which various courses can be designed, and answers questions such as:

- What are the institution's main beliefs about language education, and how are these reflected in the courses provided?
- What courses are offered to meet the needs of which kinds of students?
- What features are common to all the courses: for example, small groups, use of blended learning alongside face-to-face teaching, a focus on communicative learning objectives?
- Are there features which are common, for example, to courses for adults but not to those for children, or vice versa?

In Activity 8.1, David needs to begin by finding out from the owners what the mission of the language centre is: why does it exist? In what ways do the owners wish to help the students who attend courses and the companies that send them? He also needs to understand their values: for example, do they regard student participation and enjoyment as important parts of language education? Are they concerned about students' understanding of different cultures? Once agreed and written down, these curriculum statements can be adapted and distilled for use in public information and advertising about the institution's offer, and can be developed to form part of the guidelines for students and for staff.

A syllabus (also known as a 'course programme') is a description of a specific course or type of course that results from course design. As mentioned in the Eaquals Quality Standards, each syllabus should clearly indicate the course objectives (such as helping students to progress from A1 to A2) and content, the language usage and language forms to be taught, the learning materials to be used, and so on. For example, teachers working on a specialized course of English for nurses, as well as the students themselves, will work to a syllabus specially developed or adapted for that type of course, with objectives that are relevant to ways in which the nurses in question need to use the language and with activities and learning materials that will help them achieve these objectives. On the other hand, teachers working on general courses of English for adults open to all students with a given level of proficiency in the language would work to a syllabus common to all such courses at that level offered by the institution, with objectives probably related to the descriptors for that level in the **Common European Framework of Reference for Languages** (**CEFR**). The syllabus may have been developed some time ago, but should have been regularly reviewed in the light of feedback from students and teachers, and the progress made by students during the courses.

Once a curriculum framework has been established, the process of syllabus design itself may seem straightforward. First, the needs and expectations of the students who will be taking the course must be identified and carefully considered, then realistic objectives have to be set based on these needs, and guidelines have to be provided about how to divide up the aims over the period of the course and about the teaching materials and resources to be used. Finally, it needs to be decided how students' progress and achievement will be assessed. In David's case, he will need eventually to devise syllabuses for each type of course and each level being offered: for the general courses for adults in each language, the general courses of English for young learners, and for each of the specialized courses that companies and other organizations may require for their employees. In every case, he needs to consider how students' progress and learning will be assessed: will there be tests? If so, what kinds of tests? What kinds of assessment do students themselves need to do? Needless to say, this is quite a daunting task that may take some time, but David can probably seek help from the more experienced teachers, and he should not rush to have everything perfectly worked out before the courses start because they will probably need to be adjusted on the basis of experience.

It would be a mistake to believe that any part of this process is as simple as it sounds. Education in all fields consists of interpersonal activities involving 'mediation' of various kinds at all stages (Coste & Cavalli, 2015). Moreover, students enrolling in a given course are unlikely to all have the same needs and expectations, and teachers working on the course will naturally take different approaches to responding to these needs, however clearly defined the syllabus is.

Analysing and determining language students' needs

In principle, language courses should be designed to meet students' needs and expectations. In reality, however, many courses are designed on the basis of general assumptions about students' needs and previous experience of meeting those needs, rather than the actual needs of individuals. In an open enrolment situation, the reason for this is that it is not possible to fully understand the students' needs and expectations before they enrol and, in any case, students may not have a clear view of what their language learning needs are. Instead, they either select a course because it appears to meet their needs or, in the case of mainstream school education, because they have no real choice. The task of trying to respond to the specific needs of a given group falls to the teacher during the course. There are, however, cases where needs can and should be assessed, especially where the course is designed for a specific group of students from one organization or for students with a specific aim in mind, such as to study a degree course in the language in question.

Activity 8.2   What steps should David (from Activity 8.1) take and what means should he use to determine the language learning needs of a group of ten students that the training manager of a commercial company wishes to send for a three-week intensive course at his institutuion? The company is the national branch of a multinational mobile phone company based in Germany but which uses English for internal communications.

Determining needs in fact involves four separate steps, as indicated in Figure 8.1. Each of these steps will be explored in more detail below.

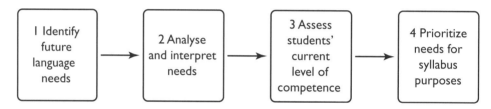

Figure 8.1 Steps in evaluating language learning needs

1 Identifying future language needs

The first step in Figure 8.1 implies that LCMs need to seek answers to at least the following questions to identify future language requirements: what do the students need to be able to do with the language, i.e. what communicative purposes are they likely to have when using it? What main topics will they be communicating about? In what situations will they be using it: with whom, in what context? How will the language be used: orally, in writing, or a mixture of both?

Such questions have formed part of needs analysis since at least the 1970s, notably where students of a language for 'specific purposes' are concerned. Munby (1978) introduced the idea of a communicative needs processor (CNP) – a procedure for processing communicative needs which takes into account the following factors and the ways in which they interact:

- the participants: who the learners are, their age, current level in the target language, other languages known, etc.
- purposive domain: the type of specific purposes for which the language will be used
- the setting: the times and places where the language is to be used
- interaction: the roles in which the participants will find themselves in terms of their status, age group, social relationships, etc.
- instrumentality: the medium of communication (spoken or written, interaction or presentation, etc.) and the channel of communication (face to face, at a distance, via digital means, etc.)

- dialect: the variety/varieties of the language the students will have to understand (and perhaps produce)
- target level of linguistic proficiency: different levels could be required for the various skills
- communicative events: what the learner will have to do with the language
- communicative key: the manner in which communication needs to be carried out, i.e. the level of formality, the register, etc.
- profile: what the student needs to be able to do.

While some of these elements may seem common sense, Munby was proposing that they each need to be taken into account and combined in order to obtain an accurate and complete analysis of future needs. Even this kind of thorough approach may not capture all the information required. Other issues may need to be explored, especially if individual students in the specialist group have different needs and language profiles. In cases like that described in Activity 8.2, there are several ways of getting at this information:

- questionnaires for the employer and/or selected students
- interviews/discussions based on the questionnaire
- observation of sample interactions in the company
- review of written documents, and so on.

It may, however, be that the employer or sponsor gives answers to the questions about language needs that are different from those provided by the students themselves, and that the answers that students provide may well differ according to their individual perspectives.

These kinds of procedures are applicable when there is a need to design a new course for a homogeneous group of students with the same specific language needs. It is, however, clear that most language courses are not designed for such groups. In a situation where a course needs to be designed for the general public, for example an evening course for adults or a summer course for junior students, this approach to needs analysis does not work. Suppositions and past experience, as well as feedback from previous courses and the insights of teachers, should be used instead. Meanwhile, in mainstream education in schools and colleges, very often the 'needs' are derived from what is specified in a national curriculum, which may or may not be based in some way on students' needs, and quite often is at least partly determined by the public examinations that students are required or intend to take.

2 Analysis and interpretation of needs

The second step of Figure 8.1 involves deciding what these future language needs mean in terms of language competence, which language skills should be focused on, and whether everyone needs to be able to cope with the same future language needs at the same level, or whether there are differences related to individual jobs or roles. For example, students of the kind referred to in Activity 8.2 may, for example, need a level of ability to read and write emails and reports in English that is higher than the ability they need to interact with others professionally in the spoken language, or the reverse may be true: more developed proficiency may be needed in the spoken language, especially if the students have to give presentations and answer questions about these. These decisions are crucial in deciding how the syllabus for the course should be organized, and what teaching approach and materials should be used.

Activity 8.3 David quickly realizes that there is a good opportunity to provide after-school classes for primary school students. At school, students up to the age of 10 have only two lessons of English a week. Parents/Carers are keen for them to have additional opportunities to learn the language after school. How should David begin to prepare the syllabuses for these courses?

In such a case as Activity 8.3, the rigorous procedure described above will not work and is not strictly necessary. Children enrolling in the courses will be of different ages and their levels of proficiency in English will vary. It is likely that David will have some experience in this area in other countries, which can be used as a starting point, but it would be wise to find out more about the English syllabus and materials used at primary schools, and very useful to get help from a teacher who has worked on after-school courses for children. This will provide a reasonable foundation for syllabuses which can be regularly reviewed in the light of accumulated experience.

Where continuing **open enrolment courses** for adults in a well-established language centre are concerned, syllabuses are generally also based on previous experience and reviewed in the light of suggestions made by teachers, or other factors that indicate a change is necessary. One thing is certain: not all students in a group at the same generic language level will have the same view of their future needs, so the syllabuses need to be flexible enough to allow teachers to cater for these differences, as well as for the differences between individuals in their rate of progress, interests, and learning styles.

3 Assessing students' current level of competence

Identifying students' language learning needs also involves assessing their current language competence: what level of competence do they already have, and what are the gaps between what they can currently do with the language and what they need to be able to do?

Activity 8.4 How could the current language competence of the students mentioned in Activity 8.2 be assessed? What tools and methods would be suitable?

Where specialized courses requested by clients are concerned, this is a key step in the analysis of needs that determines the syllabus. In this case, asking the human resources manager of the company or the students questions will not by itself uncover the necessary information. Unless the students have recently taken a formal language examination and the results are available, some kind of assessment of language competence will need to be made by the language teaching institution. Ideally, the tests and other methods of assessment used will be related in some way to the students' future language needs. This may be straightforward where competences in reading and listening are concerned, as suitable materials can be designed on the basis of the samples obtained from the company or the students. Similarly, where oral interaction is concerned, tasks can be set up that simulate the types of interaction likely to occur in real life. But there is likely also to be a need to assess students' individual general language competence to ensure that the course designed is aimed at the right level. In this case, the language institution will need to use the general tests that it has available for other students or a commercially available test that is suitable for the purpose, such as BULATS for English (see Website references).

For those wishing to enrol for an open enrolment general language course, such as the children enrolling for the after-school courses in Activity 8.3, existing language competence is generally determined by using placement tests after the courses are designed and just before they begin, such as the Oxford Online Placement Test for students of general English (see Website references). This kind of test, especially if it includes a short oral interview or oral task, helps LCMs to decide how to divide the intake of students into groups and, depending on the quality and nature of the tests, can help teachers to understand individual learning needs, but the test results do not determine the syllabus. Such placement tests generally work well unless there are too few students at certain levels to form the number of viable groups required to cover the levels of competence identified. Imagine, in the case of Activity 8.4, that most young learners are below A1, several are just above A1, and three, because of family circumstances, are at B2. Unless more higher-level students can be found, David faces a dilemma: does he tell the parents/carers of the three young learners that there is currently no course for them, or does he ask the Director to allow him to form an uneconomical group of three in the hope that more students of a suitable level will enrol at the next opportunity?

4 Prioritizing needs to create a syllabus

Returning to the group of students from the mobile phone company in Activity 8.2 (see page 104), the results from the assessments made of individual students' current language competence, combined with a clear understanding of their future needs, should provide enough basic information to enable their needs to be prioritized, as indicated at step 4 in Figure 8.1. This process will also reveal whether it is viable to teach the students as one group. If the ten students need to be divided into two or more groups for all or part of the time, this will have implications for the organization of the course due to the number of teachers and the space needed, and also for the cost to the client. The prioritization process will also need to take into account that the course is only three weeks long, which will affect which priorities can later be turned into course objectives.

Practical issues with course programmes for special 'closed' groups

Activity 8.5 Having gone through the needs analysis process for Activity 8.2, David discovers that the priorities for all students are to be able to communicate orally and by email with colleagues in other countries about work-related matters, some of which are technical (e.g. discussion of new equipment and troubleshooting problems) and some administrative (e.g. organizing and hosting visits). He also discovers that two students have a good, B1 command of English, but three others are at A1 level and lack confidence. The other five are in between these two levels.

What further questions should David ask the phone company's human resources team, and what options might he want to discuss with them?

This is where needs analysis becomes difficult, especially in a commercial environment. In the real world, human resources managers in this situation are looking for solutions, not insoluble problems. On the other hand, for reputational and commercial reasons, the institution cannot (or should not) promise what cannot be delivered. David's language centre could, however, offer three options:

1 Divide the group into two or three small groups to enable the specific priorities for the three groups to be dealt with separately: the students with a good intermediate command of English would make more progress with the specific company-related needs identified than the other groups, where the priority would be to focus mainly on developing general competence in oral communication and in simple writing.

2 Offer courses of different lengths and/or different intensity: longer or more intensive courses for the elementary students, and shorter or less intensive for the more advanced students.

3 Enable the elementary-level students to join larger groups of elementary students on the 'open enrolment' courses but, as these are mainly part-time, progress would be slower.

Other options might also be discussed, such as sending some of the students abroad for intensive study, organizing supplementary online courses, and so on. Choice of any of these options will depend on at least three factors: the priorities of the client, the budget for this language training, and the price proposed. This is why it is important during the first contact with the company to clarify what may be the outcome of the needs analysis process. In this case, the client should have immediately been made aware that it is unlikely that all ten students will have the same needs due to differing levels of proficiency. They would then be unlikely to expect the proposal to be for one group of ten.

Quality issues in curriculum and syllabus design

The previous sections have explored how the needs of students with specialized requirements can be identified in order to prepare a syllabus for them. Syllabuses for open enrolment courses are, by contrast, more usually prepared on the basis of previous experience, and often draw heavily on the learning materials that are used. Good practice is to regularly review such syllabuses in order to ensure that they continue to provide a basis for effective teaching and high-quality learning opportunities. We will now return to the question of how LCMs and their colleagues can ensure that the documentation supporting the provision of courses is of good quality, whether the courses are 'tailor-made' for specific groups on the basis of identified needs, or are designed for all-comers of a certain age or language background or level of existing proficiency, or for all-comers with clear expectations, for example that they will be prepared to take and pass a given examination. The Eaquals Quality standard specifying the existence of a statement of the institution's educational philosophy and written descriptions of its learning programmes was mentioned at the beginning of the chapter. The Eaquals scheme specifies two other quality standards for course design:

- All language course programmes are specified by levels which refer to the CEFR, and learning objectives are related to the global descriptors of CEFR levels.
- There is an academic management and coordination structure, with supporting systems, which ensure the implementation of the institution's educational philosophy.

(Eaquals Quality Standards; see Website references)

Due to the need for clarity regarding language levels, the CEFR is specified as an external point of reference. The second standard implies that centres need to have someone or more than one person in charge of language course programmes and their management. They should not just leave this responsibility to teachers.

Activity 8.6 Think about the institution you work for or last worked for. Does the institution comply with these standards? If not, what are the reasons?

Educational philosophy and values

The Eaquals Quality Standards mentioned above raise several valuable questions for language centres and their LCMs. The first concerns 'educational philosophy': language teaching institutions, like any educational institutions, and whether they are state-funded, independently funded, or commercial should have a clear mission and set of values that serve as a background to their educational work. For example, an institution may decide that its courses in various languages aim to aid personal development, international understanding, and mobility. Alternatively, the philosophy may be less general: to support students' career development and their ability to engage in communication with professional colleagues; or to enable students from abroad to complete their university studies successfully in the target language. Other aspects of the philosophy or values may involve delivering high-quality courses to meet or exceed students' expectations, and/or respecting each student as an individual with his or her own learning styles and preferences, adopting a student-centred communicative approach to language education, etc.

It is also important that the institution's general approach to language education and assessment is made clear. Currently it is common for the approach to be described as 'communicative', but what does that actually imply in practice? Does it mean that there will be little or no focus on language form such as grammar and vocabulary? Or is it that the ability to communicate is put first and the teaching and learning grammar, vocabulary, and pronunciation is closely related to communicative aims? Similarly, if an institution believes that students should take responsibility for their own learning, it needs to be clear to both teachers and students how this is reflected in the course programmes.

A further point is that this philosophy should be familiar to and supported by staff members, especially teachers, and should be made known to students. This is alluded to in a relevant Eaquals indicator, which is referred to during inspections: 'the institution's educational philosophy and pedagogic approach are sound, coherent and documented, and are familiar both to staff and—in an appropriately comprehensible form—to learners' (Eaquals, 2016a, p. 12). Thus, the task of preparing or revising curriculum documents, however concise they may be, is an important one for the LCM and fellow managers. In some institutions, staff members are involved in deciding on the philosophy and values.

The purpose and content of syllabuses

Apart from specifying the objectives of the course and its content as required by Eaquals, the syllabus may also need to state how and when students' progress and achievement are assessed, since this is an integral feature of the course. How detailed the descriptions of objectives, content, and assessment procedures are will depend on institutional systems and the needs of teachers as well as students.

Some institutions like to have syllabuses that are divided into time units—weeks for intensive courses, months for less intensive courses, or even days in some cases where the institution believes it is important for the same material to be covered on the same day of the course in all parallel classes—with sub-objectives and content specified for each unit. Institutions may wish to have a document that can be used both by students and by teachers, while others might provide a simpler and less detailed programme for students, perhaps displayed on the classroom wall or made available to them at the beginning of each week or month by email or on a web page.

The second standard of 'Course Design and Supporting Systems' in the Eaquals Quality Standards refers to the CEFR as an external reference point for specifying the language objectives and content of syllabuses. In fact, the CEFR was not originally intended to be a benchmark or standard, as is stated in its introduction:

> One thing should be made clear right away. We have NOT set out to tell practitioners what to do, or how to do it. We are raising questions, not answering them. It is not the function of the Common European Framework to lay down the objectives that users should pursue or the methods they should employ.
>
> (Council of Europe, 2001, p. ii)

But the CEFR's comprehensive 'action-oriented' approach to language use, the illustrative 'can-do' descriptors and scales that it contains, and the fact that it encompasses any (European) language (and has been translated so far into 38 languages, not all of them European), make it, in Eaquals' view and that of many other organizations, the best available reference point for describing language for teaching, learning, and assessment (as mentioned in its full title). The nearly 200 pages of text, not including the interesting appendices, are not an easy read for language teachers or their managers, who will find it easier and perhaps equally insightful to refer, for example, to the papers by Heyworth, Morrow, and others in Morrow (2004). Eaquals itself has developed numerous resources that offer familiarisation with the CEFR. It is, however, important that language educators are at least familiar with the 'global scale', the self-assessment grid (both reproduced in Appendix 3 for convenience), and the discussion of scales of illustrative descriptors and levels of proficiency, and their potential usefulness in language education (Council of Europe, 2001, pp. 24–40).

Activity 8.7   Look at the 'global scale' and the 'self-assessment grid' in Appendix 3. What do you consider to be the main advantages and possible disadvantages of relating syllabuses to the levels illustrated in the CEFR?

The key point from the Eaquals point of view is that, for institutions that wish to become members of the association, direct or indirect reference in their course programmes to the view of language learning, the levels and relevant illustrative descriptors in the CEFR indicates that the syllabuses are based on sound principles rather than only on the specific view of language learning held by their staff members or by textbook writers. The fact that providers of language examinations, publishers of textbooks, and even national governments in their immigration policies also refer to the CEFR levels has meant that language students themselves have become used to thinking about their language proficiency in terms of A2, B1, B2, and so on, rather than in terms of vague adjectives like 'elementary', 'intermediate', and 'advanced'. Some institutions may view the levels as not appropriate for their students, especially if they are mainly children, although they are still valuable reference points for their teachers. Others may consider them too broad: after all, it is hard to do justice to the wide span between elementary language competence and 'mastery' of a language in six levels. Eaquals itself has done work to overcome this limitation by proposing 'plus levels' and descriptors to bridge the gap between, for example, B1 and B2. The lack of greater specificity may also be a concern for institutions dealing mainly with students at beginner and pre-elementary levels, for example, newly arriving migrants and refugees, or the first year of language study in the mainstream school system. A further perceived disadvantage may be that it sounds as though the institution's own tried and tested system for naming and describing levels has to be abandoned. This is not the case: for example, the Eaquals standards make it clear that the levels used need to be related in a principled way to the CEFR levels, which may simply mean putting the corresponding CEFR level in brackets beside the institution's own terms. To summarize, Figure 8.2 illustrates the relevant Eaquals indicator of compliance with its standards.

> There are written descriptions of the institution's learning programmes:
> - within a framework of levels referenced to the CEFR
> - specifying practical learning objectives for each level by using 'can do' statements such as those developed for the CEFR, or statements such as 'by the end of the course learners will be able to…'
> - specifying what language knowledge and skills, for example in grammar, vocabulary, and communication skills (spoken and written) will be covered at what level
> - specifying the organization and timing of content designed to achieve the learning objectives
> - where learning programmes are learner-defined (for example in tailor-made or one-to-one teaching), there are documented procedures for carrying out a needs analysis and evidence of how this is linked to the learning programme.

Figure 8.2 Eaquals indicator of compliance (Eaquals, 2016a, p. 12)

How exactly all this is done depends on the needs of the institution, including especially its students and teachers, but also on internal policies related, for example, to the amount of autonomy teachers are allowed, whether or not the syllabus is closely related to a textbook, and whether there are practical reasons why the syllabus needs to be 'covered' within the same number of hours or weeks in all classes. One fact, however, emerges from experience within and outside Eaquals: the process of developing and organizing a syllabus or course programme, including how it is presented for teachers' use and for the information of students, is more likely to be successful if teachers are consulted and are involved in the process, and if it is also piloted and later regularly reviewed so that improvements and change can be made where necessary.

The third Eaquals standard relating to course design concerns the need for a coherent approach to academic management in this area as in the other areas described in Chapters 3–8. The relevant indicators will be referred to in Chapter 11.

Going through a process to develop a sound syllabus or course programme based on students' language needs as well as on the educational principles spelled out in the curriculum, with clear learning objectives and a more or less detailed description of the content, is already a sizeable and demanding task for any LCM. As with other such tasks, experience and consultation with colleagues are invaluable and can make it less daunting. In order to complete the job, however, systems for assessing students' learning also need to be worked out since establishing whether or not students have achieved the objectives and 'learning outcomes' described in the syllabus is crucial both for teachers, students, and the LCM.

Assessment of language learning

Assessment of learning is an integral part of teaching and learning. As mentioned above, the general approach taken to it and the principles adopted within an institution should be made clear in the curriculum document, and the actual timing and means of assessment should be specified in the syllabus. If they are not incorporated in the syllabus, the assessment policy and methods need to be clearly defined in one or more other documents.

The focus of this section is on assessment that is carried out by the institution as part of the courses it provides, not on examinations offered by public examination bodies that students may enrol for via the institution or independently.

Activity 8.8 In your experience, what types of assessment are carried out by language teaching institutions? What is the involvement of teachers in the processes related to assessment?

Course-related assessment can have at least three separate purposes, as described in Figure 8.3.

Type	Purpose – to assess:
Placement	What level of proficiency students already have in order to decide whether they are ready for a course (if a certain level is required for entry), or which course and level they should be placed in. This kind of assessment was discussed in the section concerning student needs.
Progress	How students are progressing in relation to the objectives of the course, for their information, and to enable teachers to make adjustments that take account of the individual and collective progress made.
Achievement	Whether students have achieved the necessary learning outcomes to be able to 'pass' to the next course and/or next level, and in given cases whether they can be awarded a specific certificate of achievement (for example, stating that they have reached level A2).

Figure 8.3 Purposes of course-related assessment

Aside from these main categories, course-related assessment can serve other purposes. For example, placement tests can also be diagnostic in that they may identify language areas that are problematic for students, as can progress tests, which may serve the additional purpose of motivating students. Assessment of this kind is sometimes referred to as **assessment for learning** in the sense that students can learn from the experience as well as the results of the assessment. Achievement tests, on the other hand, are more likely to be assessments of learning—an exercise to verify what or how much has been learned. This is not to say that students will not learn from achievement tests, too, especially if they are of a high quality.

Activity 8.9 David, from Activity 8.1, knows that a key part of his task as the LCM at a new language centre will be to work out procedures to enable teachers to assess the progress of their students, and for the centre to assess whether students have achieved the learning objectives specified for each proficiency level. What advice can you offer to help him do this in a methodical way?

In addition to its standards for course design in language centres, the Eaquals Quality Standards also outlines standards for assessment and certification (Eaquals 2016a, p. 14). These are expanded on below, indicating the issues that LCMs need to consider when planning and managing assessment of different types.

Assessment procedures are compatible with the institution's educational philosophy and course objectives

This standard is about coherence between the educational philosophy and approach, and the philosophy and approach behind assessment. For example, if the approach to teaching is described as 'communicative' and many teaching objectives are expressed in terms of what students can do with the language, it would be inconsistent if the means of assessment did not reflect this but concentrated only on grammar and vocabulary. In the light of this, David would need to ensure that there is consistency between the course programmes and the means of assessment related to them.

Placement procedures are appropriate to the learning context and learners' needs

As discussed at the beginning of this chapter, an important criterion related to assessment for placement purposes is how effective it is in ensuring that, for example, students' levels of proficiency in oral interaction are assessed in addition to their knowledge of grammar, vocabulary, and language use so that the assessments result in homogenous groupings of students according to level and/or specific purposes, and how efficient they are in terms of the time required for students and staff. There is a potential conflict here: LCMs need to judge how long students should have to spend being tested when they might instead be attending a lesson; and whether staff time can be made available to interview each student individually, even if only for 5 minutes. Or could oral competence be assessed in a different way?

Systems for assessing language competence provide reliable, valid, and fair means of evaluating progress and achievement in a way that is appropriate for the course and the learners

This standard brings in three key characteristics of good quality assessment which are especially relevant to assessment of progress and of achievement. The means of assessment need to be reliable. In other words, the results need to be consistent whoever is carrying out the assessment and whoever the students are. They also need to be valid in the sense that they actually assess what they are intended to assess. For example, an assessment of communicative ability in spoken English should not focus mainly on pronunciation. It does so where the student's pronunciation would interfere with communication, but there are other features of the language that are more important for effective communication such as fluency and coherence. In addition to this kind of validity, it is important that means of assessment are felt to be valid to students. Finally, fairness is essential. Assessing progress does not mean bringing in language forms and elements that are not covered by the course objective or other areas of the teaching programme.

David may have had experience of developing means of assessment for progress and assessment. If so, he will know that ensuring these criteria are met is not a simple matter. Apart from careful development procedures, teachers need to be trained to use them well, and the means of assessment need to be piloted and the results and feedback from students and teachers need to be taken into account before the assessment systems are fully implemented.

Reports and certificates issued to learners indicate their achievements in terms of the course objectives and content. They provide a reliable statement of the level achieved.

This brings us back to validity and reliability. In order for a valid and reliable certificate of achievement to be issued, the assessment(s) beforehand, which focus on whether or not a student has reached the target level of proficiency (for example, B1 at the end of a course which aims to enable students to achieve that level of proficiency) need to be a valid and reliable means of determining whether or not a student has reached 'the level' referred to in the certificate. If the certificate is based only on a teacher's subjective view, then it is less likely to be reliable.

Means of assessment

Activity 8.10 Consider the statements below. What is your reaction to them?

a The most useful, valid, and reliable ways of assessing progress and achievement during a language course are tests prepared by the institution.

b Teachers know their students best: they are in the best position to assess their progress or achievement.

c Even trained teachers of languages are not sufficiently well trained in carrying out assessments of students' learning.

Starting with statement c, it is certainly true that a majority of teachers on pre-service as well as INSET courses spend much more time being trained how to teach and support students' learning than on how to assess that learning. This is regrettable since, as previously mentioned, assessment forms an integral part of learning and can happen as part of teaching, for example when errors are being dealt with or when students are being given individual feedback on oral or written tasks. Statement b is also partly true: teachers should be the ones who best know their students, but if they do not have the right level of awareness of or competence in the principles and techniques of assessment, their assessments may be incomplete and purely subjective. A consequence of this, and doubts about teachers' ability to be objective about their students, leads to the belief reflected in statement a: tests are likely to be not just more reliable and more valid in students' eyes if prepared by the institution; they are also safer and more time-efficient. For many LCMs, relying mainly on standardized tests, including the progress tests provided in many published coursebooks, may therefore appear to be the safest and most convenient option. However, to adapt a sentiment expressed by Arnold Wesker (1960, p. 87), there is nothing wrong with tests, only there's something wrong with tests all the time. It is true that tests can come in all sorts of shapes and sizes and can be used to assess oral interaction as well as grammar and writing, but in the context of a language course, they can have a **washback effect** on teaching as teachers worry more about preparing students for their tests than about helping them to develop their language competence.

LCMs need to consider other means of assessing students' progress. These may include assessment tasks, continuous assessment, and self-assessment. Assessment tasks can be designed to assess certain communicative course objectives involving an ability to use specific language skills, vocabulary, and grammatical features. With guidance, such tasks can be used in class following standardized criteria, and teachers can develop new tasks based on agreed models. Continuous assessment involves using standard criteria to assess what students do lesson by lesson, and where they are and are not progressing. This kind of assessment also requires that teachers are trained to apply the standardized criteria and to make good use of the outcomes of such assessments. Finally, self-assessment allows students to assess themselves according to descriptors like those in the self-assessment grid in the CEFR and using portfolios such as those that follow the model of the **European Language Portfolio** (**ELP**), including one developed by Eaquals and ALTE (see Website references). The ELP model comprises a language biography, a language passport, and a dossier. An Eaquals guide to using the ELP is provided on the accompanying website to this book (www.oup.com/elt/teacher/lcm). LCMs need to think carefully about whether self-assessment can be used effectively within their course. Teachers as well as students need to fully understand its purpose and its role in learning. Any portfolio system will need to be well supported by teachers to begin with, and its use will require careful monitoring.

A combination of carefully designed ways of assessing students' progress, accompanied by standardized criteria for assessment, are more effective and more efficient, as well as potentially more reliable, valid, and fair than a single means, such as only regular tests designed by someone within the institution or by teachers themselves. A key issue for LCMs to consider is how the means of assessment will fit into the syllabus: how frequently will students' progress be assessed, and how will the focus and means of assessment relate to the course content and objectives? What kind of feedback and follow-up will there be for students? If continuous assessment is part of the system, what aspects of learning and progress will it cover, and how will teachers record the results?

To summarize, like LCMs in any language centre, David from Activity 8.9 needs to ensure that the documentation for teachers, for example the teachers' handbook and the information given to students, describes clearly what kinds of assessment are used, what purposes they serve, and when they are used. He also needs to ensure that students' expectations concerning tests and other kinds of assessment are managed. Depending on the country where the language centre is established and/or the countries where students come from, it is especially important to manage cultural assumptions: students (and their parents/carers) may assume that testing is simply a way of showing them how little they know, or is the main reason why they are taking the course, because the notion of assessment for learning and as an integral part of learning has not been part of their experience. David also has to make sure through workshops and other forms of INSET with the teaching team that assessment approaches and procedures are standardized across the whole institution, that all teachers use an agreed range of assessment types with a good balance of assessment for learning and assessment of learning, and that the ways in which feedback is given to students and results of assessment are recorded and are also in tune with the agreed approach. This may be easier for David than in established centres because he will be recruiting new teachers who are expecting to encounter systems and procedures that are unfamiliar to them. On the other hand, since no courses have yet been run, he will be relying on teachers from the locality to advise on and assist with the development process, and especially with piloting and providing feedback on the various forms of assessment.

There is much more to be said, for example about standardization training for teachers, especially those using CEFR levels and descriptors as a basis for assessment, as well as about ways of validating tests and other means of assessment, and moderation. For example, by involving more than one teacher in the assessment process, or assessing students in someone else's class. Eaquals has developed guidelines on these issues, and the Council of Europe has produced a manual for relating language examinations to the CEFR (Council of Europe, 2009).

Conclusion

This chapter has provided a short overview of LCMs' priorities and concerns in relation to student needs, curriculum and syllabus design, and assessment. It is a given that different institutional contexts and aims can impact on the decisions that have to be taken in these areas and the detail of the procedures that need to be set up. There is much more to be said about the principles that are commonly followed and the practices adopted in making these decisions and designing the relevant procedures. The third title in this series, *Language Course Planning*, will offer much more guidance and support for managers who are dealing with these complex matters.

9 MANAGING LEARNING RESOURCES AND TECHNOLOGY

Introduction

Activity 9.1

The LCM of a well-established language centre in northern Italy has recently resigned to move to a university teaching position after 15 years in his post. A new LCM, Maria, has been appointed from a smaller centre in Rome. She applied for the job because the centre is a much larger institution and offers courses in German, Spanish, and Chinese in addition to English. There are also teacher training courses.

During her interview, Maria is told that top management are concerned by negative feedback both from students and from teachers about the teaching and learning resources and equipment in the centre: students find the coursebooks used in class dated, and many of them have already used the same English books at school. The quite large 'study centre' is hardly used by students because it is full of old books, bilingual dictionaries, magazines, and audio recordings that are poorly organized. There are two computers for student use, but the exercises and activities on them are not felt to be useful. There is also unreliable internet connectivity in the school. In the teachers' room it is a similar story: there are plenty of well-worn resources, but it is hard for teachers to find what they are looking for, and many of the shelves are full of material that is almost never used. As a result, teachers generally stick to the coursebooks specified for their course. There are small CD players in most classrooms, but some of them don't work. Apart from that, there are four laptops and four data projectors that can be borrowed from the LCM's office on request, but these are rarely used because there are very few resources available on the laptops, and because of the unreliable internet connectivity. Maria has accepted the job on the understanding that a significant budget for new resources and equipment will be made available in the first year, and that she will be supported by two part-time coordinators.

How should Maria plan a project to review and upgrade the resources at the centre?

Activity 9.1 illustrates, rather dramatically, one of the most important areas of an LCM's work: managing the resources that are used by teachers and students. The project that Maria needs to plan is more complex and demanding than it would have been if her predecessor had put in place an ongoing system of maintenance, renewal, and reorganization, and if there had been a more consistent approach to collecting and dealing with feedback from students and teachers. However, it is not unusual for educational establishments to find themselves with at least one or two of the problems described in Activity 9.1 simply because the LCM's other tasks take precedence, or because management systems in this area are not well designed or not properly used.

This Chapter will consider various aspects of this task in terms of the challenges posed by selecting, organizing, maintaining, and protecting the copyright of teaching resources and equipment so that the quality of these essential resources is assured for the benefit of both students and teachers.

Challenges for LCMs in resources management

Challenge 1: Choosing main coursebooks

The first task for Maria is to review the written feedback that exists and to get more up-to-date feedback on the coursebooks which students have complained about, for example, by organizing some short focus group meetings with randomly selected students, and by getting teachers of the respective languages at meetings to make suggestions or requests for improving the situation. If what she has been told is confirmed and amplified by her own investigations, the most urgent problem appears to be with the choice of coursebooks for some of the courses. Coursebooks are often specified in syllabuses, and are sometimes the main point of reference. Syllabuses may state that, in the given period or module, a specific lesson in the coursebook provides the objectives and content. In other words, the institution is depending on the selected coursebook to define the objectives and content of its courses and, in some cases, also to provide the means of assessing students' progress. Most language coursebooks are published for a broad national or sometimes global market, and may not fully meet the specific needs of students, so there are dangers in such dependence. As illustrated in Activity 9.1, there may also be a need to replace certain coursebooks because they are outdated or are widely used in other sectors of education or for other reasons, such as how useful, flexible, or attractive the topics and activities in the books are. In any language centre or school, a time will eventually come when one or more of the main coursebooks will need to be phased out and replaced. When this is the case, syllabuses based around coursebooks also need to be rewritten, but before that, research, analysis, consultation, and piloting are needed to identify the best possible replacements. The research into what coursebooks are available and which might be suitable needs to be led by the LCM but should involve at least a few teachers, some of whom may have used different books. The research involves acquiring the relevant books, looking in detail at their contents, and comparing them with each other and the existing course objectives. The criteria for selection will depend on various factors, including whether a book is compatible with the philosophy and approach spelled out in an institution's curriculum document, and the needs, levels, and ages of the students, all of which, as mentioned in Chapter 8, had to be taken into account when designing the courses in the first place. Among other factors to consider are the cultural content, organization, attractiveness, and layout of the book. These and other criteria for coursebook and materials selection are discussed in detail in books such as Tomlinson (2011, 2013).

It is, of course, possible to organize syllabuses that do not relate closely to one coursebook but instead involve a mixture of materials taken from various sources and/or prepared by the institution itself. This poses planning and management demands of a different kind, some of which are touched on in the rest of this chapter.

Challenge 2: Deciding what other materials and resources are needed for teachers and students

One of the difficulties faced by LCMs is the sheer diversity of the resources potentially needed for teaching and learning, so a key challenge is to ensure that appropriate high-quality resources are selected and available. In this sense, Maria is in an advantageous position: a generous budget has been promised, so she may be able to weed and expand the range of resources available more quickly than would normally be the case, but deciding what to acquire is not a straightforward task.

Activity 9.2 Look at the list of some potential language teaching resources in Figure 9.1 (this does not include equipment, which is dealt with later), and add to the list if you wish. In your experience, what types of resources have proved most important and most useful to teachers and their students? What types of resources should Maria prioritize?

> **Published books:**
> - language learning coursebooks, usually in a series for different levels
> - reference books, e.g. dictionaries, grammar books, etc.
> - supplementary books for students, e.g. graded readers, exam practice books, etc.
> - supplementary books for teachers and students with activities and exercises for specific areas, e.g. vocabulary, grammar, reading and writing, communication, games, etc.
> - handbooks for teachers with techniques, ideas, discussion of theory, etc.
>
> **Online resources:**
> - websites and apps specifically designed for language practice for students
> - websites and apps intended for use by native speakers
> - news websites
> - online videos and podcasts
> - social networks such as Facebook, Instagram, etc.
>
> **Resources created or selected by teachers:**
> - pictures, posters, flash cards, maps, etc.
> - fun activities, e.g. board games
> - class sets of mobile devices, e.g. tablets
> - DVDs and CDs, video and audio material stored on mobile devices, MP3 players, USB sticks, etc.
> - software for language practice

Figure 9.1 Some language teaching resources

It is likely that readers will want to add to this list because, thanks to developments over the last few decades, many different kinds of resources are available to teachers in most of the main world languages, and new publications are appearing all the time. Teachers also have a natural desire to be able to pick and choose from what is available, and creative teachers enjoy developing their own materials from scratch, which can expand the range of resources for the centre. This wide choice creates several management challenges. In Maria's case, it will be important to review in some detail:

- what resources exactly are already available for each language, level, and course type
- what resources are already available for use by students in the study centre in print and in digital form
- which of these supplementary resources for teachers and items for students to use or borrow for their autonomous learning are not used, and the reasons for this
- where the gaps are from the point of view of the various course objectives and course lengths
- what teachers feel they need in addition to what is already available.

However, Maria would be well advised to wait until decisions have been taken about changing or keeping main coursebooks before compiling a wish list of new resources because supplementary resources should complement these coursebooks rather than duplicate them.

Challenge 3: Financial considerations

LCMs need to make decisions about what can and cannot be purchased in a given period, bearing in mind that some of the resources depend on the right equipment also being available. If there is a specific sum of money allocated to teaching and learning resources, as in Maria's case, LCMs need to find a way of selecting what should and shouldn't be bought. Some LCMs encourage teacher participation in this: having drawn up a list of what is definitely needed, as mentioned in Challenge 2, teachers can be invited to nominate titles or types of resources to be added to the list, depending on what funds are available. It is important, however, that teachers give reasons for the items suggested, and it is desirable that the team has a chance to review and discuss the list together in a meeting. Here, LCMs need to use their skills to facilitate and guide the collective decision-making process, and to make it clear that there are financial limitations and that prioritization is necessary.

If it becomes clear that it would be desirable or necessary for the centre to develop purpose-specific resources of its own, the cost of paying individuals or teams to do this needs to be carefully assessed since materials development projects can be costly in terms of time and the need to substitute teachers working on them. In addition, the ownership of the resulting intellectual property needs to be clear from the outset. In other words, if writers are paid a fee for preparing specific resources for the use of teachers at the centre, they need to know whether they have the right to publish or use the material outside the centre. The issue of copyright of internally produced materials is discussed in Challenge 8.

Challenge 4: Storage and classification

Even in language centres that have a system in place, storage and classification can still slip if it's not regularly checked. Resources can become disorganized and, in some cases, are not removed even though they become obsolete (as discussed in Challenge 5). Because of this, all too often teachers find it hard to familiarize themselves with the resources available or to find what they want quickly, which may result in the same materials being used again and again.

Clearly, in Activity 9.1, storage and classification has become a significant problem over the years. A clear and up-to-date cataloguing system is needed for physical resources, such as printed books and DVDs, and LCMs need to ensure that there are clearly labelled spaces where they can be stored in a way that is both logical and that makes them easily accessible. For **digital resources** such as worksheets, video and audio recordings stored on a computer drive, a similar catalogue is necessary and LCMs should ensure that teachers have access to the folders where the materials can be found. In addition, the catalogue of these materials needs to be compatible with the catalogue of printed materials, and perhaps printed out for quick reference. For example, LCMs can use the course types as the main organizing principle for both catalogues of resources, or the two catalogues can be merged into one, and symbols used to indicate the types of resource.

Challenge 5: Quality and relevance

Many bookcases in teachers' rooms and student libraries are half-full of resources, both published and home-made, that are hardly used or are no longer relevant. Similarly, computer drives may house obsolete digital resources that clutter up the cataloguing system, making it harder to find the right material quickly. LCMs need to find the means, at least annually, to ensure that these unused resources are removed or moved to an archive so that space can be found for new items, and so that materials can be more easily found. Teachers themselves need to be consulted during this process so that they know what is likely to be disposed of and can object if they wish to.

Challenge 6: Tracking resources

Once a cataloguing system is in place, and once any obsolete resources have been removed, the next challenge for both LCMs and teachers is keeping track of the resources that have been provided. For example, if there are class sets of certain books, teachers have to take responsibility for ensuring that the full number of them is returned. With digital resources, the problem is more likely to be accidental deletion or moving of files, but this can be overcome by having a strong and regular back-up system. When physical resources such as coursebooks are borrowed by teachers or by students, LCMs should organize a checking out and checking back in system that is quick and easy to use, and ensure that teachers use it conscientiously. In many institutions, such systems are monitored by teachers themselves; this approach can work well, or badly. The alternative is for the LCM to appoint someone to run the system, for example, by releasing a teacher from a few hours of teaching.

Challenge 7: Respecting copyright of externally produced resources

When reusing or photocopying learning materials, the authors and original sources should be acknowledged clearly. With electronic files, the title and author of any original material used can be built in, but when photocopying or scanning printed pages, the acknowledgement has to be added by hand if not already on the page. In many countries there are strict rules about acknowledgement and about how much of any book can be copied, so national regulations must be made known to teachers and followed. In some cases, institutions have licensing agreements with publishers to enable them to use digital versions of printed materials so that these can be used for certain purposes. Controlling who has copies of the full digital version, from which other copies could potentially be made, may still pose problems. Depending on national legislation, teachers need to know that they themselves may be legally liable for any breach of copyright.

Challenge 8: Respecting copyright of internally produced resources

In terms of quality, sharing, and ownership of copyright, the development of internally-produced resources is also an important consideration. There are at least two scenarios to consider. The first is when the LCM asks an individual or a small team to develop special resources for a given course type and purpose, and the institution pays them to do this work. In such cases, the issue of whether the institution or the writers, or both together, will own the copyright needs to be specified before the work begins. Logically, if the writing is paid for, the copyright is primarily with the institution, but it depends on how the institution uses it in the future. This is another area where effective management is critical: the project needs to be planned, budgeted for, managed, and monitored. Depending on the scope of the project, it may be beneficial for the materials to be designed in consultation with potential users, and for the project to include a piloting phase so that quality can be controlled.

The second scenario is when teachers of their own accord produce resources for their individual use in class. In this case, they will be 'piloting' the materials and carrying out quality control themselves. LCMs can help by first making sure that all such materials look professional and use the same institutional template when printed and photocopied, mention who the author is, and make any acknowledgements that are necessary. Guidelines for teachers in the form of a simple list of questions can help them think through the purposes, organization, and content of each worksheet before writing it. The guidelines can also suggest that teachers don't produce a worksheet just for their own use but should be prepared to allow other teachers to use it if they wish to. For various reasons, sometimes to do with self-confidence or possessiveness, teachers can be quite reluctant to share. Having a system that enables them to do this easily—for example, opportunities at teachers' meetings to introduce samples of their resources, and a folder in which electronic materials can be shared and commented on—may encourage more sharing and improve team spirit. After all, such exchanges are also ways of increasing the awareness and expertise of the whole team.

Challenge 9: Embedding resources in the syllabus

Embedding resources in the syllabus is partly to do with teacher training and development, and partly with the effectiveness and quality of actual teaching (discussed in Chapter 7), but it can also be a matter of course and syllabus design and institutional policy. Syllabuses should not simply specify what teaching and learning resources should be used, but should also indicate how they should be used and supplemented. As mentioned in the Introduction to this chapter, some syllabuses relate closely to a given coursebook and assume that it will be worked through page by page. The danger is that, instead of supporting students' learning in a creative and adaptive way, teachers simply spend their time guiding students through coursebook exercises and giving them some feedback on these. Teachers may believe that there is no need or no time to bring coursebook activities to life by relating them to students' own experiences, extending them with additional scenarios, or supplementing them with relevant other activities from supplementary books, digital materials, or worksheets. At the other extreme, where a syllabus is not related to a specific coursebook but encourages teachers to use a range of resources, students may spend their time dipping in and out of different books, handling a variety of home-made worksheets, and possibly drowning in a sea of disparate resources. An area for LCMs to consider carefully when agreeing individual development needs is the effective use of teaching and learning resources during a course and in an individual lesson. This involves achieving an optimum balance between teaching that focuses on:

- resources designed specifically for language education
- real-world resources (TV commercials, news items, songs, etc.)
- resources that students (and the teacher) bring with them—e.g. their own ideas, experiences, hopes, dreams, and lives—that can stimulate real communication in the classroom in ways that other resources cannot and can often arise naturally from activities based on language learning and real-world resources.

Activity 9.3 Most of the challenges above are referred to, in one way or another, in the Eaquals Quality Standards (see Website references) and the indicators related to 'academic resources' (see Figures 9.2 and 9.3). Match the indicators related to the three standards with the challenges. Are there any standards/indicators that refer to issues not discussed in Challenges 1–9?

> 5.1 The coursebooks or other core course materials, online learning platforms and resources, and reference materials reflect course objectives and the methodology used.
> 5.2 There is a system for monitoring learning material developed in-house.
> 5.3 All equipment and electronic connectivity is accessible and well maintained.

Figure 9.2 Eaquals Quality Standards relating to 'Academic resources' (see Website references)

> a) All course materials and resources including coursebooks, supplementary materials, reference materials, multimedia material and online learning platforms and resources are appropriate to the learners' levels and needs, the course learning objectives, and the institution's stated pedagogic approach.
>
> b) All resources are used in accordance with international copyright law. The source of all copyright material is fully acknowledged on all copies made.
>
> c) Published materials are adapted to the needs and interests of particular groups and individuals, and are used to motivate learners, and to draw out the relevance to them and their lives where possible.
>
> d) The quality—of both appearance and content—of in-house material is monitored to ensure it is appropriate for the learners, their needs, and the course learning objectives. All learning materials are in good condition and are stored/catalogued in such a way as to be easily accessed as needed.
>
> e) All equipment and academic resources are properly maintained, and connectivity (of electricity, telephone, the internet, etc.) is consistently reliable, particularly where delivery of all or part of the course is reliant on such connections.
>
> f) All equipment and academic resources are accessible in a way that meets reasonable expectations given public descriptions of such equipment and resources. There is also evidence that the resources are not just available, but regularly and effectively used. This means, for example:
> - all teachers are trained to the requisite level to use the equipment and technology available and necessary for course delivery
> - all classes/individuals have equal opportunities to learn using technological and digital teaching and learning aids available (this should not depend on being in a particular classroom or having a particular teacher)
> - where there are resources such as libraries, computer rooms, or self-access centres, these should be available in a way that is reasonable (in the institutional context) during class hours (to groups on a rotating basis, if appropriate) and/or for a reasonable period outside class hours (during breaks and/or after hours)
> - teachers have adequate access to the equipment and technology necessary for planning and preparation of teaching.

Figure 9.3 Indicators of compliance with the Eaquals Quality Standards (Eaquals 2016a, p. 16)

Managing teaching and learning equipment

This is one challenge referred to in the Eaquals standards and indicators that was not discussed above. Typically, equipment is a source of worry for managers and teachers alike because of its potential to malfunction at the worst possible time, but electronic and other equipment has become an essential resource in the language classroom. Since the nature and configuration of the equipment is constantly evolving, its use and management will not be explored in detail here. There are, however, a few general guidelines to be discussed.

| **Activity 9.4** | What general advice would you offer a recently appointed LCM, like Maria in Activity 9.1, about the acquisition and management of equipment in a language institution? |

A way of looking at this question is to think of the different ways in which equipment enhances learning. We can then break this down into different categories, the most likely of which are listed below. This will, of course, depend on the syllabuses and the resources that are required or recommended.

1 Displaying content to the whole class

Equipment for displaying content to the whole class needs to be large enough and located centrally so that it can be seen by all, durable, convenient to write and draw on, and easy to clean. It also needs to be constantly maintained and renewed when necessary. **Interactive whiteboards** (**IWBs**) have become a popular piece of equipment in education as they provide additional flexibility (such as being able to play audio content) and can, effectively, also be used as a large touch-screen computer. The cost of equipping classrooms with IWBs is, however, large, and needs to be carefully weighed against the additional benefits such devices offer.

If the cost of IWBs is out of an institution's price range, data projectors can offer many similar benefits. If a projector is fixed to the ceiling and easily connected to a portable device, this can be satisfactory from the teacher's and students' point of view. As with IWBs, however, it is advisable to install one in every—or at least several—classrooms, which is likely to be costly, rather than making a few portable projectors available to teachers to take into the classroom. A white surface to project on is also needed, and ordinary whiteboards may not be as ideal for this as a simple area of white wall beside the board.

It is worth reminding ourselves that it is possible to provide good language education with no equipment except a normal whiteboard or blackboard: hundreds of millions of students, especially school-age students, are still educated in this way around the world.

2 Playing audio

Most language education, at one time or another, involves whole classes being able to listen to audio. As mentioned above, IWBs can serve this function, but, in spite of technological advances, using such equipment is often not ideal due to a lack of sound quality. Stand-alone equipment such as a CD player or a portable amplifier for MP3 players or USB sticks, or a mobile device, is often, on its own, insufficient for a busy classroom. Inexpensive fixed solutions involving at least well-placed speakers (preferably wireless) can make a huge difference to audibility as these speakers can be connected to different mobile devices and audio equipment as technology evolves.

3 Accessing the internet

If an IWB or mobile device and data projector is used to project audio, video, and images, it can also be used to bring up internet pages and to use applications (or apps) that require internet access. This does, however, assume that the institution has invested in good and reasonably fast internet connectivity throughout the premises, which is clearly not the case in Activity 9.1.

Increasingly, students also need to access the internet for group and individual tasks in the classroom, in which case there are other considerations. Some institutions have to rotate to a space equipped with multiple computers for such work, which reduces flexibility and may make group work harder to organize. Others invest in an approach whereby each student is lent a device to use in class. This is currently a good solution, especially if the teachers' devices are equipped with an app that enables them to manage and control students' devices so that they can, for example, share content and even 'lock' the devices so students can't use them. However, cost implications can, again, be high due to upkeep and the need to replace outdated devices. For a majority of adult and adolescent students, the most flexible and easiest solution is for them to access the internet via their own mobile devices: a solution commonly referred to as the bring your own device (BYOD) approach. Apart from reducing cost, BYOD also has other advantages. For example, if the institution uses a learning platform (such as Moodle), continuity between classroom learning and autonomous learning outside the classroom can be increased and, therefore, different perspectives on 'homework' can be offered. The difficulty with this solution, however, is to create a policy which encourages students to use their devices only for language learning purposes during the lesson.

Technical support

A key management issue in all cases is to ensure that teachers, including newly appointed teachers, are well trained in the use of all the equipment and software and apps that they have access to so that they don't restrict themselves only to what they feel comfortable with. Teachers should also be trained in basic troubleshooting and problem-solving in relation to classroom equipment so that teaching and learning are not disrupted unnecessarily. Generally, a system should be in place to ensure that equipment is maintained, and that problems that arise can be dealt with quickly. An issue that affects LCMs, but which is usually outside their control, is whether a member of staff has responsibility for ensuring good and rapid technical support, or whether this is outsourced to another organization. The latter may be less costly but can mean that support is less rapidly available.

Other uses of equipment by staff members and students

Digital equipment is used for several other purposes in educational institutions and is discussed in more detail below.

a) Accessing the internet: given the increasing use of the internet in classrooms, and the fact that it is indispensable for all staff—and probably all students—to have access to it at any time, wireless hubs and routers throughout the institution are needed. The monthly cost of internet connectivity may increase if solutions with greater bandwidth and higher speeds are needed, but the equipment required is inexpensive and easy to maintain. Depending on the premises and distances between routers and extenders, professional help may be required to get this right. This affects all aspects of the institution's work so the LCM needs to make it very clear to those in charge what quality and extent of internet access is required by teachers and students.

b) Providing facilities for student study outside the classroom: many institutions have a firm and laudable belief that students, especially those on intensive courses, should be given space and facilities to work on their language and other learning outside the classroom but within the institution, and LCMs are often responsible for overseeing these facilities and ensuring that they are equipped with the necessary resources and equipment to facilitate independent learning. Increasingly, traditional student libraries are being replaced by multimedia or computer rooms, where there may also be a space for printed books, newspapers, and magazines. An advantage of this investment is that the computers or other devices provided can be linked to a network of resources intended for students to use outside the classroom and, for example, provide access to language learning software that enables students to record themselves speaking and to compare this with a recorded model. Depending on how it is organized, the multimedia room can perform functions similar to those of the former, very costly but relatively short-lived and little-used language laboratory (which can serve as an example of how technological innovations should not be too hastily adopted or promoted).

c) Providing access to specific internal networks: most institutions require at least two digital networks: one for staff and one for students. The network for staff members is likely to be divided into sections with different access and different software requirements depending on individual roles (e.g. tailored administrative software for enrolment, attendance, financial management; publishing and creative solutions for marketing and design; educational and presentation software for teachers). The separate network for student use often provides access to any proprietary learning materials and software, but it also allows communication between students and staff. Most networks are easily set up and managed via the internet, but to avoid excessive and wasteful costs, very careful and strategic planning is needed on the part of all managers to ensure that the institution has the access and communication facilities that all its stakeholders need. For example, such networks are increasingly used for recording student attendance, progress, and other records. This can work well if teachers are given access to the devices that they need and the necessary training, and have sufficient time to input the information required. So, the LCM needs to be involved in, if not responsible for, investigating and comparing solutions, consulting colleagues and students, and taking a decision in the light of this research and consultation before a change from paper-based solutions is embarked on.

d) Enabling teachers and other staff to print and photocopy: as mentioned above, however well developed an institution's educational technology is, teachers and other staff are still likely to require paper copies of teaching materials and other documents. The difficulty for teachers is that, depending on how well prepared they are, access to printers and copiers (usually now the same device) is quite likely to be required at the same time of day before, between, and after lessons. Again, LCMs need to resolve such issues as whether the quantity of copying/printing is limited for each class and/or teacher, whether the printing/copying is done by teachers themselves, whether there is a system of control over what is copied/printed, how many printers/copiers to make available and where, and how to ensure that they function well at all times.

There has been no attempt in the above discussion to be comprehensive. Expert advice on the use of technology in education, and specifically language education, is available in several books, such as Dudeney & Hockly (2014), Sharma, Barrett, & Jones (2014), Walker & White (2013).

Blended learning

In education, the term 'flipped classroom' has become popular in the current century. It implies that, instead of the teacher's main input for learning taking place in the classroom, in the form of presentations, explanations, and lectures, it is provided before the class via video or some other medium for students to watch/read before class. Class time is then used for discussion of questions and the outcomes of related assignments. Thus, the relationship between classroom time and homework is reversed, although this depends on what is understood by 'homework' in various contexts. Even in language education, the notion of flipped learning is gaining ground. Those promoting such an approach suggest that teachers can, for example, present language and provide ways of practising language and communication via a learning platform on the internet so that students can start their learning at home, thus providing extra learning time, and then focus on additional opportunities for practice, especially communicative practice and activities, such as dealing with questions, giving feedback, etc. in classroom time.

This kind of learning is becoming a key aspect of blended learning, as institutions increasingly take advantage of technology and the internet to add dimensions to the language teaching offered in traditional classrooms. These additional opportunities can form part of the learning that goes on in the institution without requiring the teacher to be available in the same way as during face-to-face learning. More often, blended learning involves students in learning activities outside the institution, including before the course begins and after it finishes. Eaquals has developed quality standards for blended language learning, which are also covered up to a point by the standards and indicators listed by Eaquals (2016b). Some samples of these parallel blended learning indicators for section 3 of the Eaquals inspection criteria on 'Course design and supporting services' are provided in Figure 9.4.

> b There are clear goals for online services designed to achieve stated learning outcomes. There is also clarity of learning pathways, menus, or hyperlinks related to learning outcomes and, where appropriate, to a needs analysis, supporting learner decisions as to what to do next. For example, lists of activities in sequence, organized by linguistic/communicative focus, or suggestions for further practice to recycle or extend learning with relevant pages should be easy to identify.
> d There are induction procedures in place to ensure staff can exploit available online tools sufficiently well to consistently deliver programme promises. These measures may include live training (face to face or by videoconference), video guides, mentoring and/or self-evaluation.
> e A member of the academic management team has considerable experience and demonstrable competence in the learning technologies in use for product delivery.

Figure 9.4 Inspection criteria on 'Course design and supporting services' (Eaquals, 2016b, p. 8)

This small selection of additional indicators gives an idea of the scope of the market research, decision-making, and planning needed before an institution can introduce blended and online learning alongside classroom-based courses.

Activity 9.5 In your view, what could be the main advantages of developing some kind of online and/or blended learning provision alongside traditional language courses? What other questions would LCMs need to ask themselves and the Director of the centre before beginning work on such a project?

The main advantages of a blended learning programme are the broader scope and greater quantity of the language learning opportunities provided, the fact that students can do their learning at times and places that suit them, and at their own speed. It is also to be hoped that students are better prepared for and able to follow up their classroom learning, as in the flipped learning approach. In other words, students do not have to be in the classroom or the institution to participate in all parts of a course provided by the institution. Depending on how many additional resources and activities are provided and whether or not these are closely linked to the progression indicated by the course syllabuses, students can spend many hours of their own time learning the language. Moreover, students are becoming increasingly accustomed to this way of learning in their other courses in secondary, vocational, and higher education. It is, however, essential that students have clear options about which learning pathways to choose to suit their learning preferences. What the potential benefits are of language courses that are exclusively available online without face-to-face or distance contact will not be discussed here as this is a specialized and controversial field of activity.

Other advantages to the institution of supplementary and online services are public relations and marketing. If students, especially those on short intensive courses, are given access to blended and online learning opportunities before they begin their course and after they finish it, a meaningful relationship is quickly established with the institution and can be maintained beyond the face-to-face course. Before the course begins, some induction and preparatory work can be provided, which will be useful when the face-to-face course starts and, after the course ends, learning can continue without interruption in the event that the student is enrolling for another course or moving on to the next school year.

Apart from the potential purposes and advantages, LCMs in consultation with the Director and members of the teaching team need to think through several other questions before decisions about such learning opportunities are taken:

- Should the blended or online learning be an integral and obligatory part of the course or an optional extra? If it is optional, this will mean that flipped learning will not work so well because only some students will engage in online learning, making life more difficult for teachers.
- Should the provision be closely linked to the syllabus and follow similar objectives, topics, and progression, or should it be quite separate and different in style and content? Or, should both types of learning opportunity be provided?
- Will the blended learning activities be assessed in any way, are there opportunities for students to check their own answers, and is any kind of feedback or follow-up to be offered by teachers? As discussed in Chapter 8, assessment is a key part of learning, and additional assessment carried out as part of blended learning will require careful organization and a time commitment by the LCM.
- Will the blended and online learning be interactive in any way, in the sense that there is online communication between students and the teacher, and among students?
- In a commercial environment, and where the provision is to be an optional extra, will students be charged an additional fee for access to the service? Where it is an integral part of the course, will course fees have to be increased to cover the costs of development and provision?
- Depending on the answers to the questions above, can teachers and other staff members create the blended or online materials and activities themselves using authoring software and an existing learning platform, or does the material need to be developed by specialists? In either case, if the project is agreed, the LCM will need to prepare and negotiate very careful specifications of what exactly the new course elements should comprise.

- What additional training is required for teachers to ensure that they can 'make the most' of the blended and online learning provision decided on? How will the LCM prepare for and organize this INSET, and who will deliver it?
- What budget is required to create the resources for the planned provision and to continue delivering and developing it? Like printed books and worksheets, these resources will need to be regularly supplemented and updated.

As Sharma (2010, p. 457) points out:

> The term "blended learning" is used both positively and disparagingly. Thus, a "1+1 is more than 2" argument assumes a positive connotation, i.e. combining the best of the teacher with the best of the technology will deliver improved learning outcomes. On the other hand, a negative connotation can be assumed where there may be no thought-through pedagogical relation between parts of the blend, so that the course may appear to lack coherence.

This remark and the very brief and selective consideration in this chapter of blended and online learning, a subject which is much more thoroughly dealt with elsewhere (see for example, McCarthy, 2016), should not deter LCMs and Directors from regularly considering what can be done to extend language learning courses in a coherent manner by adding on resources and services such as those referred to. Depending on the quality of design and content, as well as the pedagogical approach taken, the benefits can be very considerable both for students and for institutions, notably in extending the time and effort dedicated to language learning.

Conclusion

In this chapter, some of the academic and general management issues that arise in connection with teaching and learning resources, equipment, and blended learning have been explored. More change and development is taking place in these areas than perhaps in any other field of management covered in this book, which means that LCMs need to continually update themselves and to be supported by others, including their own language teaching colleagues, who are enthusiasts and explorers in one or other of these specialist areas. Such collaboration provides excellent opportunities for team building, for exploration, and for development within the institution. But, like other kinds of innovation, a methodical and strategic, as well as a consultative, approach is needed.

PART FOUR

10 MANAGING QUALITY: FEEDBACK, SUGGESTIONS, AND COMPLAINTS

Introduction

In a way, the whole book up to this point has been concerned with the management and development of quality and the LCM's role in this. This section provides an opportunity to consider in more detail what can be done specifically to focus on the assurance and improvement of the quality and the effectiveness of language courses within an institution. These easily misunderstood words were discussed at some length in Chapter 1. But it is also true that standard approaches to quality management are not necessarily appropriate to education. As Heyworth (2013, p. 286) points out:

> A review of quality in language education must look at quality both at a micro level – how can we define, implement and assess good practice in language teaching and learning at classroom level where there are practical operational aims? – and at a macro political level – is this practice contributing to achieving the social and developmental aims of its educational environment, as well as those of individual educational development? And is it contributing effectively to the cognitive development of learners? It is not clear that procedures imported from management necessarily contribute to achieving this.

Chapters 10 and 11 will discuss some practical approaches to quality management that have been found to be valuable; again, reference will be made to the Eaquals Quality Standards (see Website references).

Total quality management and the PDCA cycle

Total quality management (TQM) is an approach to quality management that dates back to some of the 'quality gurus' of the 1980s or earlier. The title of one of Armand Feigenbaum's books was *Total Quality Control* (Feigenbaum, 1983), and the phrase itself was used as the title of a book on quality by John Oakland (1988). The idea of TQM is that, instead of checking the quality of a product—such as a radio or a car—after it has been produced, as was the practice in the early 20th century, quality assurance is ongoing from the beginning of the process and is proactive. Systems are built into the production process that ensure the quality of the product at the end-point. As was seen in Chapter 1, the quality of a service such as hair styling or education is more complex than that of such products because of the intangible elements. Arguably, TQM is even more relevant to assuring this kind of quality because the service itself is a process (a lengthy one in the case of education) and so many factors involving so many interactions and elements are built into them.

A process relevant to TQM and all kinds of quality assurance is the 'plan-do-check-act' (PDCA) cycle (also known as PDSA, where 'S' stands for 'study') that dates back to work by the American 'quality guru' of the 1970s and 1980s, W. Edwards Deming, and as a result it is also known as the Deming cycle or Deming wheel (Deming, 1993, p. 132). The cycle, which features, for example, in the introduction of the well-known international standard *ISO 9001* (ISO, 2015, p. ix), is shown in Figure 10.1.

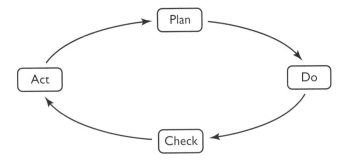

Figure 10.1 The PDCA cycle

As can be seen in Figure 10.1, the PDCA cycle involves four key stages:
- Plan: managers need to evaluate the current processes by collecting data, examining documents, etc., and then make plans to address any defects or problems they identify, and make improvements, then assess the impact of the improvements.
- Do: managers then implement the plan by making the changes planned for, and then collect data or evidence on the effects of the changes.
- Check: the third step is to examine the information and evidence collected and evaluate whether the improvements achieved the objectives established during the planning phase.
- Act: the last step is to act on the basis of the results of the first three phases, for example, by communicating the results to other staff members, and then by implementing the new processes. This is not the end of the cycle: once managers have acted, the work of planning, doing, and studying needs to continue. A related self-assessment cycle will be introduced in Chapter 11.

It is worth emphasizing that, even if overused and considered obvious by all concerned with language course management, quality must be worked on continuously and methodically: it is not an issue that can be put aside for a few months and returned to when people have time. Neither is quality the responsibility of just a few specific individuals in an organization. In general, regardless of whether an employee's job descriptions make specific reference to it or not, it is or should be a primary concern of all employees at all times. In other words, TQM and the PDCA cycle are as relevant to education as to any other service or set of products. It is therefore important that reliable quality assurance systems are in place in any educational institution.

Internal quality assurance measures

Activity 10.1 In your experience as a teacher and/or LCM, what systems are commonly used to collect evidence on the quality of language courses?

Various common procedures that are wholly or partly the responsibility of LCMs can be mentioned here. In Chapter 6, the value of observation as a tool for assessing teacher development needs was discussed, and its various other purposes, including its role in quality assurance, were explored in Chapter 7. It is clear that carefully planned observations that assess language teaching on the basis of criteria that have been established by the institution as indicators of high quality can be a useful source of evidence, but when focusing on the general quality and effectiveness of teaching it is more important that a large cross section of teachers and types of lessons are observed, even if not for a long period. The objective on such occasions is to obtain an overview of the standard of teaching and learning within the institution, not to assess individual development needs, although certain development needs that are common to several members of the teaching team may be identified in the process.

A common methodology for observations to assess teaching quality is a series of drop-in or **buzz observations**, where the observer may only see 15 or 20 minutes of teaching, backed up by a written class profile and lesson outline so that they can quickly orientate themselves. These are not quite the same as the 'surprise' observations mentioned by Bailey (2006), which were considered in Chapter 6, since teachers know at least which days or in which week to expect the observations and usually need to prepare some documentation. Eaquals and other organizations offering quality assurance services and accreditation or certification against standards use this approach. Eaquals inspectors visit as many different kinds and levels of courses as possible and aim to see a majority of teachers in action, and in smaller institutions observe all teachers, some more than once. The report on the inspection does not mention any specific classes or teachers; instead, it offers a quick overview of the types of teaching and learning observed, strong points and areas where improvement could be made, together with some recommendations if appropriate. Finally, there is confirmation that, on the basis of the evidence reviewed during the observations in this area of teaching and learning, Eaquals' Quality Standards are being complied with, are being exceeded, or are not being met.

Another common procedure is to ask students for their opinions. As pointed out in a MET project report:

> No one has a bigger stake in teaching effectiveness than students. Nor are there any better experts on how teaching is experienced by its intended beneficiaries. But only recently have many policymakers and practitioners come to recognize that—when asked the right questions, in the right ways—students can be an important source of information on the quality of teaching and the learning environment in individual classrooms.
>
> (MET Project, 2012, p. 2)

Often in language centres, students are asked to give feedback not only about the teaching but also about various aspects of the other services the institution offers, depending on the context. This can be done via online or paper surveys, and/or in face-to-face discussion with a representative cross section of students. Such systems are harder to design for younger students, especially young children. In such cases, special game-like techniques are used in class, and surveys are often made of parents'/carers' opinions instead, but the opinions will then be coloured by parents'/carers' own views on what kind of language education should be provided to their children, with perhaps little direct knowledge of what happens in the course. Ways of gathering feedback from students for quality management purposes will be explored in more detail in the next part of the chapter.

A third related and essential element in any quality approach is a robust and well-designed complaints or suggestions system; a way of receiving comments from students and other stakeholders whenever they wish to make them, which is especially the case when there is a problem from their point of view.

Activity 10.2	Marianne runs a network of language institutes in German-speaking Switzerland, which offer courses in French, Italian, Spanish, and English for company employees, younger students in vocational education, and the unemployed, as well as German courses for speakers of other languages. At present, complaints and suggestions are sometimes made to members of staff, but there is no proper system for following them up. She would like something very simple but much more thorough and quality-orientated. What would you suggest?

The borderline between a complaint and a suggestion is sometimes a fine line: the suggestion may mean that the person in question is not entirely happy but wishes to be helpful, while a complaint may be made because the person concerned is angry or upset, but it still may have been presented as a suggestion. The treatment of complaints and suggestions is best viewed as a process that needs to be clear but complete – in other words, complaints and suggestions have to be responded to in a manner that satisfies the persons concerned. Figure 10.2 indicates the main necessary steps in the process.

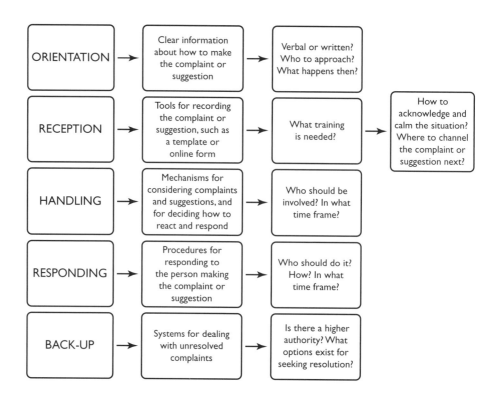

Figure 10.2 Basic components of a complaints or suggestions procedure

As can be seen from Figure 10.2, the first step is to decide who should receive complaints and suggestions, who should handle them, and who should respond to the person concerned. In Activity 10.2, with a network of schools, it may be best if the complaints and suggestions are handled centrally (for example, by Marianne in the case of those to do with the language courses) in order to ensure consistency. It would not be good for the organization if the same complaint was handled differently in different branches. For this reason, when considering how complaints and suggestions should be made, it might be better if people are asked to do this by email or by filling in a form on the institution's website. But some students and other stakeholders may wish to present their complaint or suggestion in person, so someone in each branch needs to be designated and trained to deal with them. This involves:

- having a private place to talk
- knowing how to handle typical different situations, for example people who are upset or angry and want something done immediately, as well as people who simply want to give constructive feedback
- making a written record of the complaint or suggestion
- explaining to the person concerned what will happen next and when there will be a response
- passing on the complaint or suggestion to the right person in the organization.

Once a system has been organized—and some consultation with staff members involved has taken place—the process needs to be made public, for example within the information that students receive when they first enrol, on the website, and/or in the form of a notice. Stakeholders, especially students, need to know how they can make a complaint or suggestion, who they should speak to/send their complaint or suggestion to, how long it will take to receive a response, and what will happen if they are still not happy after the complaint has been dealt with. For example, escalating it to the Director or the ombudsman of an association that the institution belongs to.

Such systems are designed not to encourage complaints, but to demonstrate that the institution is concerned about quality in all aspects of its work and is anxious to ensure that stakeholders are satisfied and can contribute their ideas and suggestions. In the case of complaints, it is also important to defuse potentially damaging situations: it is better if a student makes a complaint to the institution rather than to friends and family or on social networks, for example. Having said that, complaints and suggestions in the language education context are not frequent, and can sometimes only be inferred from student feedback at the end of a course, when it is too late so far as those students are concerned.

A fourth type of process that is recommended for any organization, but especially for educational institutions, is self-assessment. An important advantage is that it can involve various staff members and other stakeholders, not just teachers and students, and can examine all aspects of the institution's work, including internal processes and interactions. As with drop-in observations, it is first necessary to establish some clear indicators of quality, which may involve referring to external standards established by other organizations. This kind of quality management procedure will be discussed in Chapter 11.

Obtaining feedback from students

In the age of the internet we are all continually being asked to give feedback or provide reviews, and educational institutions are no exception. Language schools with a commercial orientation are just as keen as hotels and restaurants to obtain public reviews—preferably favourable ones, of course—for business reasons and to use in their publicity. But mainstream schools and institutions of higher education and adult learning also see student feedback as important. A distinction needs to be made between feedback that is mainly for marketing purposes, such as positive reviews on websites, and feedback that is carefully elicited in order truly to gauge the opinion of students and their sponsors (such as parents/carers and employers). The latter kind of feedback has to be carefully organized, gathered, and analysed if it is truly to fulfil its purpose and assist in quality management.

Activity 10.3	In the case of the Swiss network of language institutes mentioned in Activity 10.2, what kind of feedback would be relevant to collect from students? What would the headings be, and how should it be collected?

In any institution, decisions have to be taken about various issues related to the feedback being sought. The main ones are those in Figure 10.3 and are discussed in more detail below.

What?
- all aspects of the service, or selected aspects only?
- detailed or general in scope?
- different surveys for different areas?

When?
- at the end of the course, during the course, or both?
- in class, outside class, or both?

How?
- in writing, verbally, or both?
- optional or obligatory?

Method?
- rating (e.g. good = 5, bad = 0)?
- additional space for comments?
- questions with open answers?

Figure 10.3 Some decisions to be taken about gathering feedback from students

What?

The institution may want detailed feedback about all sorts of topics, ranging from the look and accessibility of its website to the way in which people are dealt with by reception staff, the teaching materials, the way the teachers work, and the classrooms and premises in general. From the LCM's point of view, the students' experience of language learning in and outside the classroom is likely to be the main concern and is also important in pointing to areas where improvements are needed, for example in teaching, assessment procedures, and in the provision of resources. It is, however, not easy to design a good survey to gather student feedback. In the type of survey used in the MET project (2012), which concerned US school education in general rather than language education, seven different headings (labelled the '7 Cs') were used to request feedback on teaching, including 'Control', 'Challenge', 'Clarify', and 'Consolidate'. Students were asked to read and rate their agreement to a variety of statements relating to each of the headings. For example, these two statements appear under 'Clarify':

- "My teacher has several good ways to explain each topic that we cover in class."
- "My teacher knows when the class understands and when we do not."

(MET Project, 2012, p. 5)

A language centre or language department is not the same as a whole mainstream school, so it may not be reasonable to consistently ask for very detailed feedback, but the principle of obtaining feedback that is relevant and differentiates students' experiences remains valid.

It is likely that the longer and more complex the survey is, the fewer people will complete it thoughtfully. As regards to the typical end-of-course survey, it may be best to ask for students' general level of satisfaction with the main aspects of the services they receive, and to ask for detailed feedback in another way at a different time. For Activity 10.3, we can assume that teaching and learning will be an important area, so there may be four or five questions on that, for example, relating to the syllabus, the teaching, the resources used, and the progress made. There may be one or two questions about interactions with other staff members and the services received, for example, reception staff providing information, or the Director of Studies and the ways in which students' progress is monitored and supported. There could also be questions about other issues such as the premises, the facilities (the library, ICT access, etc.), the website, and, of course, the price of the course. A final question in such surveys is often: How likely is it that you will recommend the course (or the institution) to other people?

| **Activity 10.4** | In a language school situated in England that offers intensive courses, what non-educational areas are likely to be covered in end-of-course surveys? |

An important additional area is likely to be accommodation if this is arranged through the school, since this is a critical part of such courses abroad, especially when homestay hosts are involved. Another important area is the social activities programme that the school offers – excursions, sport, social events, and so on. There might also be a question about the food and refreshment offered by the school and the cafeteria space. Even though these areas are not their responsibility, LCMs of such institutions need to know how the whole package offered by the language centre is viewed by students and whether there are any weak areas.

For more detailed feedback about any topic, short focused surveys can be organized at any time. For example, especially at an early stage in the course, teachers may wish to find out what their students feel about the way they are planning and teaching lessons. This could be done by a short survey using a barometer approach, as shown in the example in Figure 10.4, followed by a class activity in which students show each other their answers and discuss their opinions.

	Too little time	About right	Too much time
Pronunciation, stress, and intonation			
Grammar exercises			
Speaking activities			
Reading comprehension			
Writing practice			
Working in pairs or groups			
Repeating and practising example words and sentences spoken by the teacher			
Working on exercises in the book			
Listening to the teacher			

Figure 10.4 Sample questionnaire for classroom use

Once they begin to discuss their answers to such a questionnaire in groups, students are likely to find differences of opinion. Examples of how such questionnaires can be followed up include the following activities:

- Students try to persuade each other of their individual views on the distribution of time.
- In small groups, students work on a chart (e.g. a pie chart) in which they try to agree how much time in class should on average be spent on different aspects of language or different activities.
- The activity ends with a discussion with the teacher about individual points of view; if there are still considerable differences of opinion, the teacher can make statements, for example, about not being able to cater to everyone's different preferences, and people's learning needs and styles being different.

Used in this way, this kind of survey turns into an awareness-raising activity for students involving communicative use of the language, and a potential development opportunity for the teacher, who may decide to make some changes in the future in response to the opinions of students.

An implication for the LCM is that resources for carrying out such survey and awareness-raising activities in class with students need to be collected or added to, and the importance and different ways of incorporating such activities into the course at regular intervals should be a topic for a workshop with teachers, where ideas and experiences can be shared.

When?

End-of-course surveys are popular because it is a logical and convenient time for a global opinion to be asked for. Clearly, however, if there are any areas of dissatisfaction which students have not raised in complaints, the end of the course is too late. Many institutions also carry out limited surveys early in the course in order to establish whether, in general, students feel satisfied. Depending on the style of question, this enables them to mention issues such as whether they consider the level of their class to be right, whether they are happy with the approach taken in the course, the size of the group, and so on. These are matters that, for one reason or another, students may not raise with their teacher. If any dissatisfaction is uncovered, someone can talk to the students concerned and at least explain why things are the way they are, if not offer a solution.

In fact, as indicated in the example illustrated in Figure 10.3, during the course is a good time to explore issues of interest to LCMs and teachers in more depth with students. Having identified an area where it would be useful to have students' detailed views, such as the length and frequency of lessons in the case of the Swiss organization in Activity 10.2, or the activities offered in the social activities programme in the case of the language school in England in Activity 10.4, a student focus group can be organized. This could be done by discussion with class representatives or suitable individuals selected from different classes; these representatives would need to have time to discuss the questions to be asked in the meeting with their fellow students beforehand in order to represent the collective view as well as their own. A more usual and perhaps more reliable approach is for LCMs to take a random but representative (in terms of age, level, gender, etc.) cross section of the students whose opinions they wish to investigate, and to invite them to a discussion in which key questions can be explored. This can be done through short tasks followed by discussion or even a voting process. For example, considering a course with a total of four hours per week, students could be asked to choose their ideal length of lesson from a range of options, expressed in minutes, and the ideal frequency of the lessons. Once the selected students had had time to think about their choices and the reasons behind them, there could be a discussion to probe the arguments for and against the options, perhaps ending with a vote. The outcome may well not lead to a change in the system, and certainly no immediate change, but the institution will have explored the question carefully and can compare the opinions gathered with their own strategic and practical considerations so that any future change is based on evidence. Where appropriate, such focus groups can be followed up with wider internal surveys focusing on this question alone.

Some institutions are beginning to use technology to track opinions. For example, where students have their own accounts in an institutional network which gives them access to information, news, a communication channel with their teachers and other staff, and online learning opportunities, they can be reminded at regular intervals to register their global opinion of or feeling about their course by simply clicking on one of three or four icons. These clicks then feed into a database that enables the institution to see how individual and collective opinions change over time during the course, even if it does not explain why. This information may then lead to an initiative to explore student dissatisfaction with certain aspects of the course from time to time through individual or focus group meetings.

How?

The internet and mobile technology have changed the nature of surveying opinion and have, in some ways, made it much easier. They enable institutions and individuals to seek feedback at any time, and depending on the systems used, to immediately process the data and provide an overview of collective opinion. This is especially the case with 'yes/no' questions, multiple choice questions, and rating questions in which the respondent expresses, for example, agreement or disagreement on a rising scale. It's worth adding, with regard to this last example, that the scale should be an even number, e.g. from 1–6, as this prevents respondents simply choosing the midpoint, such as 3 on a scale of 1–5. It is also possible to add spaces for comments, although these would need to be analysed separately. Other advantages of internet-based surveys are that they can be more confidential as well as environmentally friendlier than paper versions. Confidentiality may be important where students are being asked for their opinion about teaching and the way lessons are managed.

A disadvantage of internet or email-based surveys is that they can feel and be treated as impersonal and superficial, which may encourage rushed responses that are not carefully considered, or students and their sponsors may simply not bother to respond unless there is some incentive to do so. As indicated in the examples above, face-to-face meetings are especially useful for LCMs to explore opinions in more detail, provided that the students involved are representative of wider opinion and are willing to participate actively.

Perhaps the most useful focus group meetings are those that happen between a teacher and students in class: apart from offering genuine opportunities for communicative practise in the target language, they can be used to guide teachers in their thinking about students' preferences, interests, and views about how they can best learn.

| **Activity 10.5** | Suggest two or three topics related to language teaching and learning about which teachers could ask for students' opinions, and two or three ways in which this could be done. |

The very simplest and quickest kind of feedback can be obtained after any classroom activity. Students are used to 'liking' things publicly and reacting publicly on social networks, but are perhaps less used to thinking about whether learning activities are effective for them, or indeed what the purpose of a learning activity is. It is well worth teachers' while after certain classroom activities, exercises, or tasks (if not all) to spend a minute asking or getting students to write down or discuss:

- what the purpose or aim was
- what they learned
- whether they enjoyed it and why/why not.

It is likely that opinions will differ but the responses may be quite revealing and helpful. Apps exist which enable students to answer such questions via their smartphones so that the teacher can collect their views instantly that way. Students can also be asked to 'rate' the activity on a scale of 'useful' to 'not useful', and the result can be shared immediately.

Students can also be asked for feedback on the way things are done, for example the way errors are handled. This is the kind of issue which teachers tend to have their own clear ideas about and specific habits for dealing with, but what do students think, and do they need to be made aware of the possible advantages of different approaches? Obtaining and analysing feedback of this kind, depending on how it is done, can become, an area of classroom research and requires more planning than in the previous example. First the teacher needs to decide on the range of options to be explored, for example:

- teacher correction plus student repetition
- teacher invites students to correct each other
- teacher indicates an error and asks the students to correct their own errors
- immediate correction or note-taking and delayed correction at the end of the intervention or activity.

Having explained the options and that feedback will be asked for later, the teacher then needs to use the different techniques in a balanced way over a period of two or three lessons of normal teaching before organizing a survey of opinions. Individual responses can be followed by pairs comparing their responses and whole-class discussion.

As discussed in Chapter 4, it is important to base teacher development needs and plans on evidence. Collecting evidence formally from students through surveys during and at the end of the course provides a certain kind of evidence, but obtaining feedback from students as a normal part of the teaching process, if done in a carefully planned and varied manner, can be extremely useful for teachers and have an almost immediate impact on their effectiveness and the quality of the students' learning. It is common for students to be asked for their opinions about all sorts of things such as diet, fashion, art, and music in coursebook exercises and classroom discussion. It is less common for students to be asked regularly for their views on how they are being supported in their learning. This could be a valuable topic to address in INSET, along with the related issue of 'learner training' or learning how to learn.

Who?

It needs to be remembered that there are other stakeholders whose opinions may need to be sought, depending on the types of courses offered. It may be useful to carry out short surveys or to have meetings with groups of parents/carers of younger students, especially of young children. This can be used in part as an awareness-raising exercise so that they better understand the aims of the courses and the approach being used. Then there are the representatives of employers who pay the course fees of people who work for them, which are often held on company premises. Collecting feedback from human resources or training managers who have the perspective of their own organization in mind is crucial since they may well have been involved in negotiating the aims, content length, and price of the courses in the first place. Their views and those of the students being sponsored are very informative for future contracts with the same organization and others they may be in touch with.

Conclusion

In Chapter 1, quality in the provision of services was illustrated through a scenario involving a visit to a hair salon. While language education is a more complex and longer term service, thinking of how the manager of a large salon might manage the quality of the salon's services provided by all their team of hair stylists might offer a useful parallel to this aspect of the LCM's job in an institution providing language courses. The manager would undoubtedly spend time, probably on a daily basis, observing colleagues at work and listening in to their interactions with customers, and would look at the results of the team's (and the manager's own) work. The manager would also probably have a formal or informal system for getting direct feedback from customers about their experience and their level of satisfaction with the service received. This could be done by asking them to fill in a quick survey before leaving the salon, by asking them if a link to a survey on the internet could be sent to them, or by having a quick conversation with randomly selected customers on the phone, which might sometimes lead to ideas for improvements. There would need to be a robust system for handling complaints, although this is likely to be less formal than in an educational institution as customers would most likely complain at the time or just after they receive the service. These measures would provide better evidence to base improvements on than simply relying on the manager's own and their colleagues' impressions and ideas.

This chapter has explored some ways in which LCMs can find out about the perceptions of the courses and other services being provided by organizing lesson observations to get an overview of the quality of teaching across the institution, and by taking a systematic approach to handling complaints and suggestions and obtaining feedback from students and other stakeholders. Clearly, as for the manager of the hair salon, if several types of evidence are available in addition to the formal results from the assessment of student learning, the review of quality is likely to be more comprehensive and more productive than would otherwise be the case, and the steps to further enhance quality or address shortcomings should be more clearly conceived and more effective.

11 MANAGING INSTITUTIONAL SELF-ASSESSMENT AND ACTION PLANNING

Introduction

In *Language Teaching Competences*, the first title in this series, self-assessment and reflection by language teachers about their own practice and competences was discussed at length. The issue was referred to in Chapter 5 of this book because individual self-assessment is one of the means by which teachers can reflect on their own development needs. In this chapter, self-assessment at an institutional level will be explored as a tool for quality management that can greatly help LCMs to reflect with colleagues on the development needs of their institution. While our focus here will be on self-assessment related to the planning and delivery of language courses, the practice of internal self-assessment is valid for all aspects of the functioning of an organization and has become an integral part of external quality assurance systems, such as the Eaquals accreditation scheme and the national accreditation scheme for French as a foreign language in France, *le label Qualité FLE*. Further details are provided on the websites of these bodies (see Website references). It is also seen as an important means by which organizations can assess their readiness for certification against standards such as ISO 9001. An example of a checklist designed for this purpose can be found on the BSI website (see Website references).

The concept of institutional self-assessment (or 'self-review', as it is sometimes referred to), does not contradict the concept of TQM discussed in Chapter 10, where the intention is that all of the people involved are focusing on the quality of the product or service being provided all the time. Institutional self-assessment recognizes that TQM is more an attitude of mind and a habit that individuals need to adopt in their own work. Institutional self-assessment is a more formal group activity that subjects the systems, practices, and infrastructure of the institution to regular review, but the periods between the formal self-assessments in each area are, for practical reasons, likely to be a year or more.

The aims of self-assessment at institutional level, which usually involves groups of staff members and other stakeholders, are:

- to check internally that set or agreed standards are being met in all the areas covered by the standards
- to plan corrective action to address any instances where standards are not being met

- to raise the awareness of staff members about the standards of quality the institution aims to achieve, and get their commitment to the assurance and development of quality, especially in the areas they are responsible for
- in some cases, to prepare for assessment by external auditors or inspectors working on behalf of organizations that provide certification against the standards in question, or accreditation.

Activity 11.1

Have you been involved in a self-assessment process at institutional level? If so, what activities did the process include, and who was involved?

If you have never been involved in such a process, what activities do you think a self-assessment focusing on the design and delivery of language courses should include, and who should be involved in these activities?

The process need not be complicated but it should be comprehensive and should facilitate productive and collective self-assessment, as well as encourage ongoing individual attention to quality. The suggested steps are shown in Figure 11.1, which is analogous to and has a purpose that is similar to the PDCA cycle referred to in Chapter 9. Each step will be discussed in turn in the following sections.

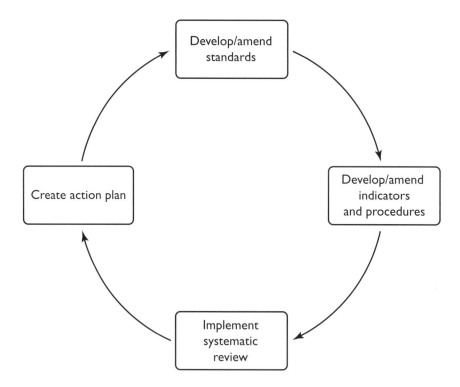

Figure 11.1 Stages in institutional self-assessment

Developing or selecting standards and indicators

Self-assessment of this kind is much easier if it is based on agreed standards. Some organizations establish their own standards, for example, through a charter which contains commitments made to customers—in this case, students—and other stakeholders such as their employees. It is recommended that LCMs sit down with a consultative group and specify the standards which an institution intends to be governed by, that cover all its activities; these should include both those which are customer-facing and those which are internal. It is, however, easier and perhaps more useful to base internal standards on external benchmarks proposed by standard-setting bodies. This is one of the reasons why organizations of all kinds opt to seek certification against one or more of the very large range of standards that have been developed by ISO and CEN (*Comité Européen de Normalisation*; the European grouping of national standards bodies that are members of ISO). Another reason why institutions opt for certification or accreditation by external bodies is because these bodies set public standards against which the work of the institution can be assessed independently, thus providing reassurance for clients. The same standards can also be used for self-assessment, and can be added to, adapted, or further specified for internal self-assessment purposes so that the work and context of the institution can be properly taken into account and reviewed.

Examples of standards relevant to language education provided by Eaquals were given in Chapters 8 and 9, and will be referred to again below. Standards are simple descriptive statements of what is expected, for example: 'the quality of course delivery consistently provides opportunities for effective learning' (Eaquals Quality Standards, see Website references). This is one of five Eaquals standards relating to teaching and learning. In the case of Eaquals, these standards are accompanied by ten indicators that are used to verify that the five standards are being met. One indicator relevant to this particular standard is 'Teaching quality is high, and clear learning opportunities for all learners are apparent in the classroom' (Eaquals, 2016a, p. 10), but other indicators guide inspectors in seeking further evidence that this standard is met. Thus, while standards may be sufficient as public statements of what an institution aims consistently to achieve in terms of quality, on their own they are not sufficient for self-assessment purposes: the indicators are extensions to the standards, the purpose of which is to answer the question: how can I tell whether this particular standard is being met, or that a set of standards for a given area of activity are being complied with? In the case of Eaquals, additional sets of indicators are provided to enable inspectors and internal assessors to establish whether levels of excellence beyond normal compliance are being achieved. These points of excellence are recorded in the inspection report provided to institutions afterwards and can be highlighted in promotional materials.

Although it is one of very few organizations that have set standards applicable to any kind of language education wherever it is delivered, Eaquals is not the only organization that offers verification against standards relevant to language learning.

One or two other international bodies do so, including ISO itself. Several national associations which are Associate Members of Eaquals have also established such standards at national level, some of them not unlike those provided by Eaquals – for example, Optima Bulgaria, QUEST Romania, PASE in Poland, and AISLi in Italy. Other bodies in the UK, Canada, USA, Australia, and France provide standards specifically for centres offering intensive courses for students coming from abroad. If an institution decides to adopt standards proposed by one of the external bodies, their first task will be to investigate and research these bodies and their standards in order to decide which is most suitable and whose standards are based on values which are close to those the institution itself upholds. The next task will be to check whether the institution actually meets the relevant standards. Self-assessment is the best way of doing this.

Adopting such standards does not automatically mean seeking external certification or accreditation: with ISO standards, for example, the intention is that users of the standard can choose third party certification or a 'first party attestation of conformity', which means that the provider has gone through a process to check that its services (or products) meet the requirements of the relevant standard.

Implementing a systematic review

Activity 11.2 Refer back to the Eaquals standards and indicators for academic resources in Chapter 9 (see page 126). What procedures would be suitable for carrying out an internal assessment of the extent to which these are being complied with? Who should be involved?

A simple first step is to turn the indicators into a checklist to stimulate checking and reflection on whether the standards are being complied with and how well, and if not, where there are shortcomings and how they can be addressed. In this case, the checklist might look like the sample in Figure 11.2.

As can be seen in Figure 11.2, instead of simply asking themselves whether or not each indicator is complied with, users of the checklist need to think carefully about whether any improvements are possible. Agreeing on the appropriate grade requires consideration of the indicators from different perspectives. Figure 11.2 is just one way in which such a checklist or questionnaire can be laid out. Eaquals has its own Self-Assessment Handbook for institutions thinking about applying for accreditation by Eaquals. This takes a simpler approach by focusing on the standards themselves rather than the indicators, as shown in Figure 11.3.

Academic resources – indicators	Grade*	Comments on grade	Action that can be taken
All course materials and resources including coursebooks, supplementary materials, reference materials, multimedia material and online learning platforms and resources are appropriate to the learners' levels and needs, the course learning objectives, and the institution's stated pedagogic approach.			
All resources are used in accordance with international copyright law. The source of all copyright material is fully acknowledged on all copies made.			
Published materials are adapted to the needs and interests of particular groups and individuals, and are used to motivate learners, and to draw out the relevance to them and their lives where possible.			
The quality—of both appearance and content—of in-house material is monitored to ensure it is appropriate for the learners, their needs and the course learning objectives. All learning materials are in good condition and are stored/catalogued in such a way as to be easily accessed as needed.			
All equipment and academic resources are properly maintained, and connectivity (of electricity, telephone, the internet, etc.) is consistently reliable, particularly where delivery of all or part of the course is reliant on such connections.			
All equipment and academic resources are accessible in a way that meets reasonable expectations given public descriptions of such equipment and resources. There is also evidence that the resources are not just available, but regularly and effectively used. Examples of this can be seen in the rows below.			
All teachers are trained to the requisite level to use the equipment and technology available and necessary for course delivery.			
All classes/individuals have equal opportunities to learn using technological and digital teaching and learning aids available (this should not depend on being in a particular classroom or having a particular teacher).			
Where there are resources such as libraries, computer rooms or self-access centres, these should be available in a way that is reasonable (in the institutional context) during class hours (to groups on a rotating basis, if appropriate) and/or for a reasonable period outside class hours teachers have adequate access to the equipment and technology necessary for planning and preparation of teaching.			
*GRADE	**NA** = not applicable	**0** = significant problems	**1** = indicator partially met, but work is needed	**2** = still room for improvement	**3** = indicator fully met, no further work needed

Figure 11.2 Indicators of 'Academic resources' (Eaquals, 2016a, p. 16) adapted as a self-assessment checklist

5	Academic resources
5.1	The coursebooks or other core course materials, online learning platforms and resources, and reference materials reflect course objectives and the methodology used.
5.2	There is a system for monitoring learning material developed in-house.
5.3	All equipment and electronic connectivity is accessible and well maintained.

Figure 11.3 Indicators of 'Academic resources' (Eaquals, 2014, p. 13)

Here, users are asked to explain in their own words how a given standard is complied with, rather than considering whether and to what extent each indicator is applicable. It is for the managers in an institution, including especially the LCM, to decide how detailed and analytical they wish the self-assessment process to be. Clearly, the larger the number of standards and indicators, the longer the process of self-review will take, but true quality often lies in the detail of systems and the way these are applied, and, for example, in actual interactions between staff, especially teachers, and students, so there are also benefits in a more detailed analysis.

Whichever standards and indicators are chosen, adapted, or written as a point of reference for self-assessment, it is possible that they will need to be added to or amended over time. This is because institutions often add to or change their courses, resources, and facilities. So, LCMs need to consider after each cycle of the self-assessment whether any standards or indicators relating to course provision have become redundant and whether additions are needed.

There are many ways to approach the self-assessment exercise, and those selected will depend on the circumstances of a given institution, how many staff members are involved in the process, their availability, and the time available. Two important points are worth making. First, there is no need to try to cover all the standards the institution wishes to comply with within one long exercise: different areas will require the involvement of different people, including different managers, and some areas may need to be tackled more urgently than others or may be harder to organize at certain times. Second, while it is desirable to involve as many members of staff as possible in one way or another, it is not necessary and probably not feasible to involve all those with an interest in the area all the time. It is, however, important that everyone understands that the internal self-assessment is taking place, what its purposes are, and how it will be organized. It is equally important that all staff members are informed about its progress and the outcomes, including in areas that they are not normally involved in. It is not good for self-assessment to be seen as essentially a management exercise which others are not involved in: the more people that can participate in reflecting on the questions posed by the indicators, the better it is for team engagement in quality assurance. Moreover, people will bring in different information and express different points of view.

Simple steps that LCMs can follow in self-assessment focusing on an academic programme are:

- To ensure that everyone is familiar with the standards that the institution wishes its activities and its internal processes to be governed by. This should automatically form part of the induction of new staff members, and regular reference to the standards ensures that they are regularly thought about; if the standards used are those set by an external body, staff members need to know about that organization and its values, and why their institution wishes to be linked to it.

- To introduce the topic of institutional self-assessment at a staff meeting, or circulate an email or post an item on the institution's social networking page about it. People need to understand what self-assessment actually means in this context, what the purpose is, and how the process might affect them. It is best if staff members have an opportunity to ask questions and to discuss the advantages and implications at this time.

- To announce, and if possible consult on, how the process is going to be conducted: which areas will be looked at first? Who will be involved in each area? What will they have to do? How will staff be kept informed? These are questions that need to be discussed openly and, where appropriate, consulted on. Depending on the situation, it may be relevant to ask for volunteers to be involved in the different sections, but it is also important to ensure that the relevant people are included.

- To make sure that each part of the process, for example each area of assessment and the group involved in it, is tightly managed. LCMs need to have clear guidance, a well-defined time frame, and to know what kind of reporting back is required, but there also needs to be some room for initiative as to how to do their work, who else to consult, etc.

Activity 11.3 Think of the institution where you are working or one where you have worked in the past. You are asked to assess whether and to what extent the indicators relating to academic resources (above) are applicable there. What information would you need in order to do this, and who would you need to consult?

Like other areas related to language courses, the area of academic resources is particularly complex because the resources are evolving all the time in quantity and quality. Some common resources were listed as part of Activity 9.1 (see page 119), but in any given institution the balance between these different types, the amount of resources that are in digital form, and the quantity and quality of home-made materials available will vary considerably. It is obvious that those involved in selecting resources and managing them need to be involved at some point, and if there is a person supervising a media centre or library facility, they should also be consulted. But the key stakeholders in academic resources are the teachers who use them for teaching purposes and the students who use them in their language learning. The LCM needs find an opportunity to consult at least some students in order to check the applicability of indicators a), c), and f) ii and f) iii (Eaquals, 2016a, p. 16). This may be best done in a focus group, as discussed in Chapter 10, but since it is likely that different classes use different resources, consulting students from three or four different classes separately might be more useful. Teachers will also need to be consulted about these indicators, and their views are definitely needed on indicators d), e), f), i), and f) iv (Eaquals, 2016a, p. 16). In this case, even if not all teachers respond, a short online survey with short follow-up interviews might be the best way to elicit their views.

This illustrates another point about self-assessment within an institution. It can be done very thoroughly by gathering as much relevant evidence as possible, which in this case might need to include evidence gathered by physically inspecting the resources, including those only available in digital form, and some lesson observation to see how resources are used; but, where such a thorough approach is not feasible, a less time-consuming and exhaustive approach can be taken to evidence gathering. The difference is in the quantity and probably the usefulness and reliability of the evidence collected. The key thing is what happens next: analysing the evidence, reflecting on it and coming to conclusions about the extent to which the indicators apply and the standards are complied with, and equally importantly, what can be done to improve things further.

The bigger picture

The example of academic resources has been used simply to illustrate what is meant by institutional self-assessment and how it can be organized in such a way as to have beneficial side-effects for the whole institution and the team or teams working in it. As was mentioned, areas can be handled one at a time, or several areas can be reviewed within a given period. The areas covered by the Eaquals Quality Standards (see Website references) are:

1. Management and administration
2. Teaching and learning
3. Course design and supporting systems
4. Assessment and certification
5. Academic resources
6. Learning environment
7. Client services
8. Quality assurance
9. Staff profile and development
10. Staff employment terms
11. Internal communications
12. External communications

Activity 11.4	Imagine you are an LCM of a language teaching institution, and are organizing a fairly comprehensive self-assessment exercise focusing on academic issues, using the Eaquals areas and indicators (or similar ones) as a point of reference. What order would you plan to handle the areas in? Which do you think would be hardest to review?

A way of thinking about this is to consider the trajectory of a student in an institution. A key issue is whether external communications via websites and publicity give a true picture of the academic services being provided. Advertising and the descriptions provided on the website and elsewhere may be the main reason why students select the institution. That information needs to be reflected in the reality of their course and the other services they receive. Having made their choice, students would begin their experience of client services when enrolling and entering the institution for the first time, as well as when wanting services other than the course itself (such as accommodation, excursions, or use of facilities for independent study). The 'teaching and learning' area follows, and would lead to 'course design and supporting systems', 'academic resources', the 'learning environment', and then to 'assessment and certification'.

Many of these areas also affect teachers, and with them in mind it is important to consider the areas of 'staff profile and development' and 'employment terms', as well as 'quality assurance', which includes observation and other measures to assess and develop quality, and, of course, 'internal communications'. In their own way the areas are all complex, but the most complex in terms of evidence gathering and evaluation of the evidence collected are likely to be 'teaching and learning', 'course design and supporting systems', and 'assessment and certification'.

Creating an action plan

The main purpose of self-assessment is first of all to verify that standards are being met, or identify areas where this is not the case, and secondly, even where standards are being complied with, to identify areas where further improvement is desirable. Following the reports on self-assessment in each area, LCMs should be able to see any shortcomings listed and recommendations made where action must be taken in order to achieve the goal of compliance, as well as where further development would be valuable. The recommendations may be idealistic or not even feasible for financial or other reasons, but the analysis of the evidence collected should indicate the problem areas. It may be worthwhile engaging in some simple intuitive (rather than researched) 'importance – performance' analysis along the lines proposed by Martilla & James (1977) for the field of marketing. This is most easily understood through the diagram in Figure 11.4.

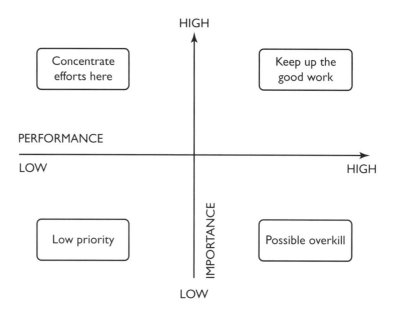

Figure 11.4 Importance–performance grid (Adapted from Martilla & James, 1977, p. 78)

The message is that the most urgent action, and the most effort, needs to be invested in areas which are seen as important by customers – in this case, depending on the area, students and their sponsors, or staff members (the internal customers), and where 'performance' in terms of quality and effectiveness is low. On the other hand, areas which are not so important but where standards are being met or exceeded need less effort, or have possibly received too much attention in the past. The plan needs to specify at least the following:

- the indicator that is to be focused on, and where there is a shortcoming (or more than one)
- what should be done to address this, and what it is likely to cost in terms of time and money
- who should be responsible for the action required – possibly more than one person or a group
- when the action should be completed.

This can be laid out as a set of proposals in a simple table, as in Figure 11.5.

Problem/ opportunity	Action proposed	Likely cost	Time needed	Who	Deadline

Figure 11.5 Template for action planning

Bearing in mind the need to keep team members informed and involved in the process, rather than simply presenting and managing the plan, it is important first to consult on it at a draft stage, especially with those involved in its implementation, but also, as regards the proposed action, with those who were involved in the self-assessment and who may have suggested different solutions to the problem or opportunity for improvement. It may be that those consulted have better ideas or are unexpectedly able and willing to contribute to the work needed, and at least they will continue to feel engaged in the process. In the LCM's areas of responsibility, there is also an important difference between creating an action plan for sensitive areas, such as teaching, which may focus on the need for more professional development for teachers, or changes in behaviour or some of the practices they use, and those areas such as resources, where the focus is not so much on people but on physical and online materials and how they are organized, used, and renewed. Clearly, it is not the purpose of institutional self-assessment to demotivate staff members, but rather to engage them in the ongoing process of enhancing quality in all areas, so feedback and action planning need to be handled especially carefully where teachers and other staff are directly affected by the proposed actions.

Adjusting standards and indicators

It is unlikely that LCMs and other managers will instigate a review of a given area or several areas more often than once or twice a year, unless there is particular concern requiring more intensive follow-up. In a year, quite a lot can change: new procedures may have been introduced and certain activities may have been discontinued or changed. So, before starting a new cycle of institutional self-assessment, it is important to review the standards and indicators used, especially if they are internal standards, to check that they are all still relevant, and to consider whether any additional standards are needed for new areas. As mentioned earlier, it is good to involve teachers and other staff members in the review and amendment of standards and indicators as part of the ongoing effort to involve them in scrutinizing the quality of their own work and the work of the institution.

Conclusion

This chapter has concentrated on using standards developed by the institution, or standards developed by an external body and adopted or adapted by the institution, as a means of reinforcing quality management. While inspection and certification by an external body may be very worthwhile, ongoing internal quality assurance is essential as a means not only of checking that standards are being maintained but as an engine for involving the whole team in reflecting on quality and specifically on where improvements can be made that will make the language education experience more effective for students and more satisfying for those who provide it. The LCM's commitment may be to the success of the institution they work for and to the effectiveness of the courses being provided, but from a professional point of view, working as a team on new initiatives can lead to even higher quality in the delivery of courses, and the raising of standards can generate an energy and a sense of collegiality that are themselves great contributors to the success and satisfaction of the team.

12 FINAL CONSIDERATIONS

Introduction

The topics dealt with in this book cannot fully reflect the complexity and pressure that comes with the role of the LCM. The nature of the role is hard to capture because of the fact that each different context and institution, each teaching team, and each cohort of students have distinct impacts on the work and life of the person employed as an LCM. But the topics and suggestions in this book highlight and seek to offer advice on many of the common challenges faced by the LCM, and help with the sheer diversity encompassed by the role.

The complexity of the LCM's role

Within a single day, it is likely that the LCM will need to grapple with issues related to teaching and the support of teachers, course design, assessment, resources, human resources, and student welfare, as well as with time-consuming administrative tasks and financial matters. In larger organizations, the LCM may also be working with coordinators or assistants who are responsible for specific syllabuses, areas of work, or branches of the organization, which adds another dimension to the complexity of the LCM's role. The fact that the LCM is often the interface between the head of the institution and the teaching team, and has to further the global and, in many cases, commercial objectives of the institution while trying to assure the pedagogic well-being of students and teachers as well as the quality of language learning also implies additional personal and professional competence and a special sensitivity to the needs of others. The job can be very demanding and stressful at times, but can also often be satisfying and rewarding. As in other parts of life, balance and the ability to maintain a positive outlook are key.

As discussed in Chapter 1, it may be useful to compare the role of teacher, a role which most LCMs have had during their careers, with that of the LCM. Teachers work at what is often described as the 'chalk face': they are preoccupied with delivering one or several courses lesson by lesson so as to help the students they work with learn the language or subject in question. They draw on the institution's resources to prepare, manage, and monitor classroom activities that suit the specific needs and preferences of the various groups they work with, juggling all of the challenging details that that involves. It can be tiring, if often satisfying and occasionally exhilarating or exasperating work, and there is little time left over to think of the bigger picture of the institution's mission and its current and future development. By contrast, LCMs need a much broader view. They need to be aware of and to manage what is going on across the whole course programme: are students learning and satisfied with the teaching they are experiencing? Are teachers doing what is expected of them, giving their best, and also developing professionally? Are the resources and systems in place to ensure that teachers and learners have everything they need to do their work? Am I doing all that I need to be doing to prepare for future courses and meet the expectations of the institution? In each case, if not, what should I be doing about it? These are some of the questions running subconsciously or consciously through the minds of LCMs while they deal with day-to-day interactions with students and staff, and with their administrative work. Thus, LCMs and the teaching team have joint responsibility for the effectiveness and quality of the various courses: teachers at a micro level and LCMs from a holistic perspective.

The LCM's professional development

LCMs themselves are indeed often so preoccupied with day-to-day administration, the welfare of students, and the professional support and development of the teaching team that they overlook or forget to reflect on and plan their own development. Moreover, many LCMs have been promoted from being teachers in the same institution, and may have only had a brief formal induction before taking up their duties. If they are lucky, they receive some practical support and advice from their predecessor in the role, or from the Director, but specific and systematic training is seldom provided in the essential skills and know-how required for the job. General management training, for example, however short-term, would be a useful way of preparing for the job, as would a course in basic principles and good practice in the management of human resources. Even short face-to-face or online courses in management are expensive and institutions are unlikely to spontaneously offer this kind of development opportunity to their managers. Nevertheless, LCMs should not be shy about requesting such training or training in other specialist areas, such as language testing and assessment, ICT, or time management from their employers, many of whom will be sympathetic to the idea of at least sharing the cost of course fees and allowing time away from the workplace for training, and some of whom will see the value of such 'upskilling' to the institution.

Apart from formal training and induction, it is important that LCMs also take some time to reflect on their own development needs by asking themselves in which areas of their work they lack confidence or feel less effective, and where they wish to further develop their skills and knowledge. In many organizations this will be covered during the appraisal process, in a way that is analogous to that discussed in Chapter 7 for teachers. The LCM's appraisal meeting is normally with the Director or a senior manager, who, like LCMs before appraisals with teachers, should provide some questions for reflection before the meeting, including questions about the areas of responsibility where the LCM feels they have done well and is confident and strong, and those where they have felt less successful. The senior manager leading the appraisal will no doubt provide their own feedback on the LCM's work so far, and this may be in tune or at odds with the LCM's self-assessment. Either way, alongside setting objectives for the coming period and seeking feedback from the LCM about the way they are managed, the appraisal should include discussion of the LCM's professional development needs and wishes, and there should be discussion about how and by whom this will be supported and monitored. LCMs should, however, not feel they have to wait until the appraisal meeting before raising their concerns or asking for support, and in some contexts where appraisal is not used or is irregular, it is important to ensure that the professional development of the LCM is given attention by top management.

Depending on needs, time, financial constraints, and personal preferences, professional development can take many forms, ranging from the management courses mentioned above to mentoring and coaching sessions, informal exchanges with LCMs in other institutions, and attending occasional conferences. As with teachers, the responsibility for pursuing professional development is with the LCM and some of it is likely to be autonomous. Where it is feasible, LCMs should not hesitate to get involved in areas of classroom or action research, materials development, or other projects that are of interest to them and relevant to the institution's needs, perhaps in collaboration with the coordinators they work with. Professional and personal development are never-ending processes, and each experience, even less agreeable ones such as dealing with difficult teachers or dissatisfied students, can lead to some valuable learning.

Promoting a positive climate

As was mentioned more than once in the foregoing chapters, for the benefit of the whole institution as well as in the interests of the personal and professional well-being of the LCM, it is essential to create and maintain working relations and an atmosphere in the staffroom that is positive and productive. This does not mean simply acceding to teachers' or students' requests on every occasion in order to pacify them. Rather, it has to do with people being treated courteously without 'fear or favour', knowing clearly what is expected of them, and feeling able to ask for help and support when they need it. The implication is that LCMs need to be frequently available and accessible, professional in all their dealings, willing to consult and acknowledge the expertise of others, but firm and frank when necessary. If they have assistants working with them (such as an Assistant Director of Studies) the roles of these people, who are most likely to be still working part-time as teachers, need to be made clear, and they need to work according to the same guiding principles as the LCM. In other words, LCMs must lead by example, and strive to ensure that the atmosphere created by their management of the course programme and the teaching team, and their assistants if they have any, is positive, professional, and leads to good outcomes for all concerned.

Conclusion

In educational institutions, whether they are mainstream schools, colleges, universities, or commercial language centres, top management has responsibility for establishing the mission and setting the global objectives and overall climate. It is, however, those managers with direct responsibility for ensuring that the courses delivered are of a high standard and that students are given effective and productive opportunities to learn who, through their efforts, have most power and the greatest responsibility to ensure that the quality of the education provided is genuinely high and that the learning resulting from it meets students' own individual needs and develops their potential. Although at times it may not feel that way, the LCM's role carries with it great potential to bring benefits to students, the institution, and society in general.

APPENDIX 1

THE EUROPEAN PROFILING GRID

TRAINING AND QUALIFICATIONS

Development phase	1.1	1.2	2.1	2.2	3.1	3.2
Language proficiency	• is studying the target language at tertiary level • has achieved B1 proficiency in the target language	• is studying the target language at tertiary level • has achieved B2 proficiency in the target language	• has gained a B2 examination certificate in the target language and has oral competence at C1 level	• has gained a C1 examination certificate in the target language or: • has a degree in the target language and proven proficiency at C1 level	• has gained a C2 examination certificate or: • has a degree in the target language and proven proficiency at C2 level	• has a language degree or C2 examination certificate plus a natural command of the target language or: • has native speaker competence in the target language
Education & Training	• is undertaking preliminary training as a language teacher at a teacher training college, university, or a private institution offering a recognized language teaching qualification	• has completed part of her/his initial training in language awareness and methodology, enabling her/him to begin teaching the target language, but has not yet gained a qualification	• has gained an initial qualification after successfully completing a minimum of 60 hours of documented structured training in teaching the target language, which included supervised teaching practice or: • has completed a number of courses or modules of her/his degree in the target language and/or language teaching pedagogy without yet gaining the degree	• has a degree in the target language with a language pedagogy component involving supervised teaching practice or: • has an internationally recognized (minimum 120 hour) certificate in teaching the target language	• has a degree or degree module in teaching the target language involving supervised teaching practice or: • has an internationally recognized (minimum 120 hour) certificate in teaching the target language and also: • has participated in at least 100 hours of further structured in-service training	• has completed a master's degree or degree module in language pedagogy or applied linguistics, involving supervised teaching practice if this was not part of earlier training or: • has a postgraduate or professional diploma in language teaching (min. 200 hours course length) • has had additional training in specialist areas (e.g. teaching the language for specific purposes, testing, teacher training)

Assessed Teaching	• is gaining experience by teaching parts of lessons and sharing experience with a colleague who is providing feedback	• has had experience of being supervised, observed, and positively assessed while teaching individual lessons • has had experience of running teaching activities with small groups of students or fellow trainees ('micro-teaching')	• in initial training, has had a total of at least 2 hours of successful documented, assessed teaching practice at at least two levels • in real teaching has been observed and had positive documented feedback on 3 hours of lessons	• in training, has had a total of at least 6 hours of successful documented, assessed teaching practice at at least two levels • in real teaching has been observed and had positive documented feedback on 6 hours of lessons at three or more levels	• has been observed and assessed for at least 10 hours during teaching practice and real teaching at various levels and with different types of learner, and has received positive documented feedback on this	• has been observed and assessed for at least 14 hours during teaching practice and real teaching, and has received documented feedback on this • has been assessed as a mentor or observer of less experienced teachers
Teaching Experience	• has taught some lessons or parts of lessons at one or two levels	• has own class(es) but only experience at one or two levels	• has between 200 and 800 hours documented unassisted teaching experience • has taught classes at several levels	• has between 800 and 2,400 hours documented teaching experience: • at various levels • in more than one teaching and learning context	• has between 2,400 and 4,000 hours of documented teaching experience, including: • at all levels except C2 • in several different teaching and learning contexts	• has at least 6,000 hours documented teaching • has taught in many different teaching and learning contexts • has experience of mentoring/training other teachers

The European Profiling Grid © EAQUALS 2013 – Brian North, Galya Mateva, Richard Rossner and the EPG Project 2011–2013

KEY TEACHING COMPETENCES

Development phase	1.1	1.2	2.1	2.2	3.1	3.2
Methodology: knowledge and skills	• is learning about different language learning theories and methods • when observing more experienced teachers, can understand why they have chosen the techniques and materials they are using	• has basic understanding of different language learning theories and methods • can select new techniques and materials, with advice from colleagues • can identify techniques and materials for different texts	• is familiar with language learning theories and methods • is familiar with techniques and materials for two or more levels • can evaluate from a practical perspective the suitability of techniques and materials for different teaching contexts • can take into account the needs of particular groups when choosing which methods and techniques to use	• is well acquainted with language learning theories and methods, learning styles and learning strategies • can identify the theoretical principles behind teaching techniques and materials • can use appropriately a variety of teaching techniques and activities	• can provide theoretical justification for the teaching approach being used and for a very wide range of techniques and materials • can use a very wide range of teaching techniques, activities and materials	• has a detailed knowledge of theories of language teaching and learning and shares it with colleagues • can follow up observation of colleagues with practical, methodologically sound feedback to develop their range of teaching techniques • can select and create appropriate tasks and materials for any level for use by colleagues
Assessment	• can conduct and mark end of unit tests from the coursebook	• can conduct and mark progress tests (e.g. end of term, end of year) when given the material to do so • can conduct oral tests when given the material to do so • can prepare and conduct appropriate revision activities	• can conduct regular progress tests including an oral component • can identify areas for students to work on from the results of tests and assessment tasks • can give clear feedback on the strengths and weaknesses identified and set priorities for individual work	• can select and conduct regular assessment tasks to verify learners' progress in language and skills areas • can use an agreed marking system to identify different types of errors in written work in order to increase learners' language awareness • can prepare for and coordinate placement testing	• can design materials and tasks for progress assessment (oral and written) • can use video recordings of learners' interactions to help them recognize their strengths and weaknesses • can apply CEFR criteria reliably to assess learners' proficiency in speaking and writing	• can develop assessment tasks for all language skills and language knowledge at any level • can apply CEFR criteria reliably to assess learners' proficiency in speaking and writing at all levels and help less experienced colleagues to do so • can create valid formal tests to determine whether learners have reached a given CEFR level • can run CEFR standardization

Lesson and course planning	• can link a series of activities in a lesson plan, when given materials to do so	• can find activities to supplement those in the textbook • can ensure coherence between lessons by taking account of the outcomes of previous lessons in planning the next • can adjust lesson plans as instructed to take account of learning success and difficulties	• can use a syllabus and specified materials to prepare lesson plans that are balanced and meet the needs of the group • can plan phases and timing of lessons with different objectives • can compare learners' needs and refer to these in planning main and supplementary objectives for lessons	• can plan a course or part of a course taking account of the syllabus, the needs of different students and the available materials • can design tasks to exploit the linguistic and communicative potential of materials • can design tasks to meet individual needs as well as course objectives	• can conduct a thorough needs analysis and use it to develop a detailed and balanced course plan that includes recycling and revision • can design different tasks based on the same source material for use with learners at different levels • can use analysis of learner difficulties in order to decide on action points for upcoming lessons	• can design specialized courses for different contexts that integrate communicative and linguistic content appropriate to the specialism • can guide colleagues in assessing and taking account of differing individual needs in planning courses and preparing lessons • can take responsibility for reviewing the curriculum and syllabuses for different courses
Interaction management and monitoring	• can give clear instructions and organize an activity, with guidance	• can manage teacher-class interaction • can alternate between teaching the whole class and pair or group practice giving clear instructions • can involve learners in pair and group work based on activities in a coursebook	• can set up and manage pair and group work efficiently and can bring the class back together • can monitor individual and group activities • can provide clear feedback	• can set up a varied and balanced sequence of class, group, and pair work in order to meet the lesson objectives • can organize task-based learning • can monitor learner performance effectively • can provide/elicit clear feedback	• can set up task-based learning in which groups carry out different activities at the same time • can monitor individual and group performances accurately & thoroughly • can provide/elicit individual feedback in various ways • can use the monitoring and feedback in designing further activities	• can set up, monitor, and provide support to groups and individuals at different levels in the same classroom working on different tasks • can use a wide range of techniques to provide/elicit feedback

The European Profiling Grid © EAQUALS 2013 – Brian North, Galya Mateva, Richard Rossner and the EPG Project 2011–2013

Appendix 1

ENABLING COMPETENCES

Development phase	1.1	1.2	2.1	2.2	3.1	3.2
Intercultural competence	• understands that the relationship between language and culture is an important factor in language teaching and learning	• is learning about the relevance of cultural issues in teaching • can introduce learners to relevant differences in cultural behaviour and traditions • can create an atmosphere of tolerance and understanding in classes where there is social and cultural diversity	• understands and is able to take account of relevant stereotypical views • can use own awareness to expand students' knowledge of relevant cultural behaviour, e.g. politeness, body language, etc. • can recognize the importance of avoiding intercultural problems in the classroom and promotes inclusivity and mutual respect	• can help learners to analyse stereotypical views and prejudices • can integrate into lessons key areas of difference in intercultural behaviour (e.g. politeness, body language, etc.) • can select materials that are well matched to the cultural horizon of learners and yet extends this further using activities appropriate to the group	• can use web searches, projects and presentations to expand own and learners' understanding and appreciation of intercultural issues • can develop learners' ability to analyse and discuss social and cultural similarities and differences • can anticipate and manage effectively areas of intercultural sensitivity	• can use her/his extensive knowledge of intercultural issues when this is appropriate to assist less experienced colleagues • can develop colleagues' ability to deal with cultural issues, suggesting techniques to defuse disagreements and critical incidents if they arise • can create activities, tasks, and materials for own and colleagues' use and CAN seek feedback on these
Language awareness	• can use dictionaries and grammar books, etc. as reference sources • can answer simple questions about language that are frequently asked at levels she/he is teaching	• can give correct models of language form and usage adapted to the level of the learners at lower levels • can give answers to language queries that are not necessarily complete but that are appropriate for lower level learners	• can give correct models of language form and usage appropriate for the level concerned, except at advanced levels (C1-2) • can give answers to questions about the target language appropriate for the level concerned, except at advanced levels (C1-2)	• can give correct models of language form and usage, for all levels up except at C2 on almost all occasions • can recognize and understand the language problem that a learner is having • can give answers to questions about the target language that are appropriate for the level concerned except at C2	• can select and give correct models of language form and usage on almost all occasions at all levels • can answer almost all language queries fully and accurately and give clear explanations • can use a range of techniques to guide learners in working out answers to their own language queries and correcting their errors	• can always give full, accurate answers to queries from students about different aspects of language and usage • can explain subtle differences of form, meaning, and usage at C1 and C2 levels

| Digital Media | • can use word-processing software to write a worksheet, following standard conventions
• can search for potential teaching material on the internet
• can download resources from websites | • can create lessons with downloaded texts, pictures, graphics, etc.
• can organize computer files in logically ordered folders | • can use software for handling images, DVDs, and sound files
• can use any standard Windows/Mac software, including media players
• can recommend appropriate online materials to students and colleagues
• can use a data projector for lessons involving the internet, a DVD, etc. | • can set and supervise online work for learners
• can use software for handling images, DVDs, and sound files | • can train students to select and use online exercises appropriate to their individual needs
• can edit and adapt sound and video files
• can show colleagues how to use new software and hardware
• can coordinate project work with digital media (using, for example, a camera, the internet, social networks)
• can troubleshoot most problems with classroom digital equipment | • can train students to use any available classroom digital equipment (IWB incl.), their mobiles, tablets, etc. profitably for language learning
• can show colleagues how to exploit the teaching potential of available digital equipment and internet-based resources
• can design blended learning modules using a learning management system e.g. Moodle |

The European Profiling Grid © EAQUALS 2013 – Brian North, Galya Mateva, Richard Rossner and the EPG Project 2011–2013

Appendix 1

PROFESSIONALISM

Development phase	1.1	1.2	2.1	2.2	3.1	3.2
Professional conduct	• seeks feedback on her/his teaching practice and other work • seeks advice from colleagues and handbooks	• acts in accordance with the mission and regulations of the institution • liaises with other teachers about students and lesson preparation • acts on trainers' feedback after lesson observation	• welcomes opportunities to share class teaching (team-teach) with colleagues at one or two levels • acts on feedback from colleagues who observe her/his teaching • contributes to the institution's development and good management and reacts positively to changes and challenges in the institution	• welcomes opportunities to be observed by managers and colleagues and receive feedback on teaching • prepares for and participates actively in professional development activities • actively participates in the development of the institution and its educational and administrative systems	• acts as mentor to less experienced colleagues • leads training sessions with support from a colleague or when given material to use • observes colleagues and provides useful feedback • when the opportunity arises, takes responsibility for certain projects related to the development of the institution	• creates training modules for less experienced teachers • runs teacher development programmes • observes and assesses colleagues who are teaching at all levels • organizes opportunities for colleagues to observe one another
Administration	• completes routine tasks like taking the attendance register, giving out / collecting / returning materials	• delivers required plans and records of lessons correctly completed and on time • marks homework and tests efficiently	• handles marking and report writing efficiently • keeps clear, well-organized records of lessons • hands in documents and feedback by time requested	• handles administrative tasks around the job efficiently • anticipates regular but less frequent tasks and completes them in good time • deals with students' issues, enquiries, feedback appropriately	• coordinates administrative tasks with others; collates information, reports, opinions, etc. if asked to do so • takes responsibility for certain administrative tasks such as organizing teachers' meetings, gathering, analysing, and reporting on end of course feedback, etc.	• acts as course coordinator if asked to do so • liaises with enrolment dept / finance dept / sponsors / parents, etc. as necessary • contributes actively to the design or review of administrative systems

The European Profiling Grid © EAQUALS 2013 – Brian North, Galya Mateva, Richard Rossner and the EPG Project 2011–2013

APPENDIX 2

SAMPLE QUESTIONNAIRE FOR COMPLETION BEFORE, DURING, AND AFTER AN APPRAISAL MEETING

Name of teacher: _____

Name of manager: _____ **Date of appraisal meeting:** _____

GENERAL COMMENTS

What aspects of your work over the past period have you found most satisfying? Why?	
Have you found any aspects of your work over this period frustrating or difficult? If so, which and why?	
Notes on discussion (agreed between LCM and teacher):	

SPECIFIC COMMENTS ABOUT TEACHING – please comment briefly on each of the following:

Your students, and the feedback received from them	
Your students' progress as indicated by results of formal and informal assessment	
The course programmes/syllabuses	
Teaching and assessment resources, including equipment	
General workload	
Other (please add)	
Notes on discussion (agreed between LCM and teacher):	

PROFESSIONAL AND CAREER DEVELOPMENT – please comment briefly on each of the following:

Your self-assessment and the discussion of it	
Your experiences of lesson observation by others (managers, mentor, peers, etc.), and its usefulness to you	
Your experiences of observing lessons given by others (mentor, peers, etc.) and yourself, and its usefulness to you	
Your agreed individual professional development objectives for the period, and additional objectives decided by you	
Your individual professional development steps and activities in the period	
Your progress towards your individual development objectives, and the impact of this on your teaching	
Areas you want to include in your individual professional development plan for the next period, and the support you think you will need	

Group professional development and INSET activities that you have participated in: their usefulness to you, and suggestions for the future	
Other comments on professional development and the support provided by the institution	
Your career aspirations: what would you like to be doing in five years' time? What opportunities would you like the institution to offer you?	
Notes on discussion (agreed between LCM and teacher):	

GENERAL FEEDBACK AND SUGGESTIONS FROM THE TEACHER

The institution as a whole and its work	
Specific systems and the way they function	
The way the LCM works with you and teachers in general (also other managers)	
Collaborating with other teachers and non-teaching staff	
Terms and conditions of employment for you and other teachers	
[other headings can be added]	
Notes on discussion (agreed between LCM and teacher):	

GENERAL FEEDBACK FROM THE MANAGER

Your work, including non-teaching work, in the period	
Your professional development	
Your collaboration and interaction with colleagues	
Your general approach and attitude	
Feedback from others	
[other headings can be added]	
Notes on discussion (agreed between LCM and teacher):	

MANAGER'S OVERALL SUMMARY:

TEACHER'S COMMENT ON THE SUMMARY AND THE MEETING:

Manager's signature:	**Teacher's signature:**

APPENDIX 3

CEFR LEVELS: GLOBAL SCALE

Proficient User	C2	Can understand with ease virtually everything heard or read. Can summarise information from different spoken and written sources, reconstructing arguments and accounts in a coherent presentation. Can express him/herself spontaneously, very fluently and precisely, differentiating finer shades of meaning even in more complex situations.
	C1	Can understand a wide range of demanding, longer texts, and recognise implicit meaning. Can express him/herself fluently and spontaneously without much obvious searching for expressions. Can use language flexibly and effectively for social, academic and professional purposes. Can produce clear, well-structured, detailed text on complex subjects, showing controlled use of organisational patterns, connectors and cohesive devices.
Independent User	B2	Can understand the main ideas of complex text on both concrete and abstract topics, including technical discussions in his/her field of specialisation. Can interact with a degree of fluency and spontaneity that makes regular interaction with native speakers quite possible without strain for either party. Can produce clear, detailed text on a wide range of subjects and explain a viewpoint on a topical issue giving the advantages and disadvantages of various options.
	B1	Can understand the main points of clear standard input on familiar matters regularly encountered in work, school, leisure, etc. Can deal with most situations likely to arise whilst travelling in an area where the language is spoken. Can produce simple connected text on topics which are familiar or of personal interest. Can describe experiences and events, dreams, hopes and ambitions and briefly give reasons and explanations for opinions and plans.
Basic User	A2	Can understand sentences and frequently used expressions related to areas of most immediate relevance (e.g. very basic personal and family information, shopping, local geography, employment). Can communicate in simple and routine tasks requiring a simple and direct exchange of information on familiar and routine matters. Can describe in simple terms aspects of his/her background, immediate environment and matters in areas of immediate need.
	A1	Can understand and use familiar everyday expressions and very basic phrases aimed at the satisfaction of needs of a concrete type. Can introduce him/herself and others and can ask and answer questions about personal details such as where he/she lives, people he/she knows and things he/she has. Can interact in a simple way provided the other person talks slowly and clearly and is prepared to help.

(CEFR, 2001, p. 24)

APPENDIX 4

CEFR SELF-ASSESSMENT GRID

		A1	A2	B1
UNDERSTANDING	Listening	I can recognise familiar words and very basic phrases concerning myself, my family and immediate concrete surroundings when people speak slowly and clearly.	I can understand phrases and the highest frequency vocabulary related to areas of most immediate personal relevance (e.g. very basic personal and family information, shopping, local area, employment). I can catch the main point in short, clear, simple messages and announcements.	I can understand the main points of clear standard speech on familiar matters regularly encountered in work, school, leisure, etc. I can understand the main point of many radio or TV programmes on current affairs or topics of personal or professional interest when the delivery is relatively slow and clear.
	Reading	I can understand familiar names, words and very simple sentences, for example on notices and posters or in catalogues.	I can read very short, simple texts. I can find specific, predictable information in simple everyday material such as advertisements, prospectuses, menus and timetables and I can understand short simple personal letters.	I can understand texts that consist mainly of high frequency everyday or job-related language. I can understand the description of events, feelings and wishes in personal letters.
SPEAKING	Spoken Interaction	I can interact in a simple way provided the other person is prepared to repeat or rephrase things at a slower rate of speech and help me formulate what I'm trying to say. I can ask and answer simple questions in areas of immediate need or on very familiar topics.	I can communicate in simple and routine tasks requiring a simple and direct exchange of information on familiar topics and activities. I can handle very short social exchanges, even though I can't usually understand enough to keep the conversation going myself.	I can deal with most situations likely to arise whilst travelling in an area where the language is spoken. I can enter unprepared into conversation on topics that are familiar, of personal interest or pertinent to everyday life (e.g. family, hobbies, work, travel and current events).
	Spoken Production	I can use simple phrases and sentences to describe where I live and people I know.	I can use a series of phrases and sentences to describe in simple terms my family and other people, living conditions, my educational background and my present or most recent job.	I can connect phrases in a simple way in order to describe experiences and events, my dreams, hopes and ambitions. I can briefly give reasons and explanations for opinions and plans. I can narrate a story or relate the plot of a book or film and describe my reactions.
WRITING	Writing	I can write a short, simple postcard, for example sending holiday greetings. I can fill in forms with personal details, for example entering my name, nationality and address on a hotel registration form.	I can write short, simple notes and messages relating to matters in areas of immediate need. I can write a very simple personal letter, for example thanking someone for something.	I can write simple connected text on topics which are familiar or of personal interest. I can write personal letters describing experiences and impressions.

B2	C1	C2
I can understand extended speech and lectures and follow even complex lines of argument provided the topic is reasonably familiar. I can understand most TV news and current affairs programmes. I can understand the majority of films in standard dialect.	I can understand extended speech even when it is not clearly structured and when relationships are only implied and not signalled explicitly. I can understand television programmes and films without too much effort.	I have no difficulty in understanding any kind of spoken language, whether live or broadcast, even when delivered at fast native speed, provided I have some time to get familiar with the accent.
I can read articles and reports concerned with contemporary problems in which the writers adopt particular attitudes or viewpoints. I can understand contemporary literary prose.	I can understand long and complex factual and literary texts, appreciating distinctions of style. I can understand specialised articles and longer technical instructions, even when they do not relate to my field.	I can read with ease virtually all forms of the written language, including abstract, structurally or linguistically complex texts such as manuals, specialised articles and literary works.
I can interact with a degree of fluency and spontaneity that makes regular interaction with native speakers quite possible. I can take an active part in discussion in familiar contexts, accounting for and sustaining my views.	I can express myself fluently and spontaneously without much obvious searching for expressions. I can use language flexibly and effectively for social and professional purposes. I can formulate ideas and opinions with precision and relate my contribution skilfully to those of other speakers.	I can take part effortlessly in any conversation or discussion and have a good familiarity with idiomatic expressions and colloquialisms. I can express myself fluently and convey finer shades of meaning precisely. If I do have a problem I can backtrack and restructure around the difficulty so smoothly that other people are hardly aware of it.
I can present clear, detailed descriptions on a wide range of subjects related to my field of interest. I can explain a viewpoint on a topical issue giving the advantages and disadvantages of various options.	I can present clear, detailed descriptions of complex subjects integrating sub-themes, developing particular points and rounding off with an appropriate conclusion.	I can present a clear, smoothly flowing description or argument in a style appropriate to the context and with an effective logical structure which helps the recipient to notice and remember significant points.
I can write clear, detailed text on a wide range of subjects related to my interests. I can write an essay or report, passing on information or giving reasons in support of or against a particular point of view. I can write letters highlighting the personal significance of events and experiences.	I can express myself in clear, well-structured text, expressing points of view at some length. I can write about complex subjects in a letter, an essay or a report, underlining what I consider to be the salient issues. I can select style appropriate to the reader in mind.	I can write clear, smoothly flowing text in an appropriate style. I can write complex letters, reports or articles which present a case with an effective logical structure which helps the recipient to notice and remember significant points. I can write summaries and reviews of professional or literary works.

(CEFR, 2001, pp. 26–27)

GLOSSARY

The definitions provided here reflect the way in which the terms are used in this book. In some cases, the terms have different definitions when used in other contexts.

action research: An approach to professional development in which teachers focus and reflect on specific teaching and learning questions, with the aim of improving both their students' and their own learning. It often includes *classroom research*.

appraisal: The process of assessing employees' performance against expectations and/or objectives, often done through annual or more frequent meetings between individual employees and their managers.

assessment for learning: Procedures for assessing progress and outcomes in language learning that simultaneously help students to learn more or reinforce their learning.

assessment of learning: Procedures, including tests, that aim to check whether a student or a group of students has made progress in their language learning or has reached a certain level of proficiency. Apart from tests, these procedures can include task-based assessment, teachers' continuous assessment, self-assessment by the student, etc. which may also contribute to learning.

authoritarian: Used when describing, for example, managers who adopt a style of communication that assumes strict obedience from staff members who report to them, whatever the nature of the decision.

authoritative: Used when describing, for example, managers who have credible authority over staff members due to the quality, clarity, and style of their actions and communications.

blended learning: A combination of face-to-face classroom methods with computer-mediated activities that often take place outside the classroom.

buddy system: A system of induction which involves an experienced member of staff being available to help a new member of staff to adjust to the new organization for a specific period of time.

buzz observations: These are normally observations of a short part of a lesson which give the observer a 'snapshot' of the teacher's work. The time is usually not arranged in advance; the teacher only knows that they will be observed at some point during the day, or week.

classroom research: Research done by teachers in their own or colleagues' classrooms with the aim of investigating issues such as the effectiveness of teaching, the reactions of students, and their learning. It is often part of *action research*.

Common European Framework of Reference for Languages (CEFR): An internationally recognized framework which provides descriptors (can-do statements) of language ability, prioritizing the communicative competences of learners of foreign languages at different levels (A1, A2; B1, B2; C1, C2).

competence: The ability to deploy a combination of relevant knowledge, skills, and attitudes in an appropriate way to successfully accomplish a given task, such as language teaching.

continuing professional development (CPD): The activities, experiences, and events that help groups and individuals (in this case, teachers and others in the field of language education) to develop professionally during the course of their employment.

curriculum: The overall description of the aims, content, length, organization, methods, and evaluation of educational courses offered by an institution; contrasts to *syllabus*.

descriptor: A statement that describes a given competence, area of knowledge, or characteristic, usually presented in organized groups within a framework, such as the Common European Framework of Reference for Languages.

digital resources: Digitized content (text, graphics, audio, and video) for teaching that can be transmitted over the internet or computer networks.

Eaquals: An international association of institutions and people that provide or are involved in language education. Eaquals, which stands for 'evaluation and accreditation of quality in language services', is committed to fostering excellence in language education.

effectiveness: The impact of a service or activity like teaching, i.e. the extent to which it supports and furthers learning, or in the case of management, for example, the extent to which the manager's work has the desired outcomes for the organization and the quality of its courses.

European Language Portfolio (ELP): A document in printed or electronic form that enables students of languages to assess themselves against the self-assessment scales in the CEFR and to record their progress and achievements in language learning.

European Profiling Grid (EPG): A framework of descriptors available in a number of different languages to enable language teachers to assess themselves and create a 'profile' of their competences, and to help managers and teacher trainers assess language teachers. It is also available in interactive form online as the e-Grid.

focus group: A group of customers or students who are asked to participate in a discussion of specific issues related to the quality of a service, such as a language course.

grievance: A serious complaint by an employee about any issue relating to work, such as the employer organization, the terms and conditions of work, the behaviour of work colleagues, etc.

ICT: Information and communication technology, a term commonly used to refer to digital resources and equipment such as those deployed in teaching.

indicator: A phenomenon, event, or state of affairs that provides evidence of or a measure for something else; for example, the quality of teacher training courses.

induction: Processes and information that help orientate a new employee or student in an institution.

in-service training (INSET): Training offered to an employee, for example, in the form of workshops or short courses that they can attend while working.

inspector: An official representing an external body who visits an institution, such as a school, to check the quality of its services and facilities against standardized criteria.

interactive whiteboard (IWB): A large interactive display that connects to a computer and projector and can be written on with a digital pen.

language course manager (LCM): Anyone in any kind of educational institution who has management responsibilities related to delivering language courses, for example, Directors of Studies, level coordinators, heads of language departments, Academic Managers, etc.

mentee: A less experienced or new employee, in this case, a teacher, who receives support and guidance in their teaching from a mentor.

mentor: An experienced teacher, tutor, or academic manager who shares knowledge, skills, and perspectives to support the personal and professional growth of a less experienced teacher.

mentoring: A scheme or practice in an institution in which experienced teachers work as mentors with less experienced teachers, or teachers who need support with their development, by helping them to plan their lessons, by observing and giving feedback on their teaching, by giving them advice, etc.

needs analysis: A procedure for identifying why students need or wish to study the target language, including the purposes for which they will use it and in what specific contexts.

observation scheme: A system for organizing lesson observations, often of more than one kind, in an institution.

open enrolment course: A course which is open to any student who fulfils the entry requirements, such as having the right level of proficiency in a language.

performance management: The processes and systems used to evaluate how well employees are doing their job, and to encourage them to continue their efforts and improve their performance further.

professional development: The professional learning and growth that teachers achieve in the process of gaining experience and knowledge and reflecting on their teaching; see also *continuing professional development (CPD)*.

professional learning: The professional knowledge, skills, and so on which results from experience, from CPD and teacher development, etc.

quality assurance: Procedures and practices that are designed to verify that quality standards are being met, and to improve things if they are not.

quality control: Checking of quality, usually done by external inspectors or agencies (or internally, after components and products have been manufactured).

recruitment: The process which includes advertising jobs, reviewing applications, and the interviewing, selection, and appointment of successful applicants.

reflection: The experience of considering the implications of something that has happened, a decision to be made, or a state of affairs. In this book, the term is used mainly to describe the kind of thinking teachers do after assessing themselves, following a lesson, or when thinking about their own development needs.

self-assessment (institutional): A process by which an institution reviews all or certain aspects of its work with the aim of checking whether improvements are necessary so that quality can be further improved.

self-observation: The process of reflecting systematically on one's own teaching after (and sometimes during) a lesson. Teachers can make notes and discuss their self-observation with someone else. It is, of course, far easier to do this if a video or at least an audio recording has been made.

shortlisting: The drawing up of a list of candidates who may be suitable for an advertised job and therefore should be interviewed.

stakeholders: People with a specific interest or involvement in something, such as an institution providing language education. Stakeholders in this case can be students, teachers and other staff, and also parents/carers, employers, local authorities, etc.

standards: Statements that specify the conditions necessary for a service (or product) to be at an agreed level of quality.

syllabus: A written outline and summary of the content of a course of instruction and the order in which skills and/or knowledge are to be taught, usually including an indication of how the time should be allocated; contrasts to *curriculum*.

teacher's log: A written record of a teacher's experiences in the classroom and during professional development, professional learning, and so on, often including the teacher's thoughts and feeling about these experiences.

teacher development: The gradual development of individual teachers' competences, including knowledge, skills, and attitudes, that takes place as a result of training, day-to-day teaching experiences, interaction with colleagues, training events, etc. See also *professional development*.

teacher trainers: Professionals who deliver teacher education and teacher training courses.

total quality management (TQM): A management system used by some organizations to ensure that everyone in the organization focuses on quality all the time in order that the organization continually improves.

washback effect: The impact that assessment has on classroom teaching and learning. It can be positive (e.g. when students understand through assessment where their weaknesses are and how to improve in these areas), or negative (e.g. when students only focus on learning what they think will be tested).

WEBSITE REFERENCES

Chapter 1

Oxford Dictionaries
https://en.oxforddictionaries.com

ASQ Quality Glossary
http://asq.org/glossary/q.html

Chapter 2

European Profiling Grid (EPG)
www.epg-project.eu/the-epg-project

Chapter 3

Skype
www.skype.com

Adobe Connect
http://www.adobe.com/products/adobeconnect.html

Chapter 4

Measures of Effective Teaching Project
http://k12education.gatesfoundation.org/resources (Search for 'Learning about Teaching'.)

Chapter 5

European Profiling grid: e-Grid
http://egrid.epg-project.eu

The EAQUALS framework for language teacher training and development
www.eaquals.org/our-expertise/teacher-development/the-eaquals-framework-for-teacher-training-and-development

Moodle

https://moodle.com/moodle-lms

Chapter 6

The Eaquals quality standards

https://www.eaquals.org/our-members/become-a-member/accredited-membership/the-eaquals-quality-standards

Teachers Media International: From good to outstanding

http://www.teachers-media.com/series/from-good-to-outstanding

Chapter 7

The Chartered Institute of Personnel and Development (CIPD)

http://www.cipd.co.uk/hr-resources/factsheets/performance-management-overview.aspx

Chapter 8

BULATS

www.bulats.org

Oxford Online Placement Test

https://www.oxfordenglishtesting.com

Common European Framework of Reference (CEFR)

www.coe.int/t/dg4/linguistic/Cadre1_en.asp

The European Language Portfolio (ELP)

www.coe.int/t/dg4/education/elp

Chapter 9

The Eaquals quality standards

https://www.eaquals.org/our-members/become-a-member/accredited-membership/the-eaquals-quality-standards

Chapter 11

Eaquals accreditation

https://www.eaquals.org/our-members/become-a-member/accredited-membership

ISO 9001 Quality management: Self-assessment checklist (the International Organization for Standardization)

https://www.bsigroup.com (Search for 'resources for ISO 9001' and download the 'ISO 9001 self-assessment checklist'.)

ISO 29991:2014(en): Language learning services outside formal education – Requirements (the International Organization for Standardization)

https://www.iso.org/obp/ui/#iso:std:iso:29991:ed-1:v1:en

Le label Qualité FLE

http://www.qualitefle.fr/en/pro/rubriques/le-label-en-details-14511

REFERENCES

Bailey, K. M. (2006). *Language teacher supervision: A case-based approach.* Cambridge: Cambridge University Press.

Blumberg, A., & Jonas, S. (1987). Permitting access: The teacher's control over supervision. *Educational Leadership, 44(8),* 58–62.

Borg, S. (2016). *Enhancing the impact of in-service training.* Presentation at TESOL Arabia, Dubai, United Arab Emirates. Slides retrieved May 2016 from http://simon-borg.co.uk/wp-content/uploads/2013/03/Borg-TESOL-Arabia-Plenary-2016-slides.pdf

Christison, M. A., & Stoller, F. L. (2012). *A handbook for language program administrators, second edition.* Burlingame, CA: Alta Book Center Publishers.

Coste, D., & Cavalli, M. (2015). *Education, mobility, otherness: The mediation functions of schools.* Strasbourg: Council of Europe. Retrieved December 2016 from http://www.coe.int/t/dg4/Linguistic/Source/LE_texts_Source/LE%202015/Education-Mobility-Otherness_en.pdf

Council of Europe. (2001). *Common European Framework of Reference for Languages.* Cambridge: Cambridge University Press. Retrieved November 2016 from http://www.coe.int/t/dg4/linguistic/Cadre1_en.asp

Council of Europe. (2009). *Relating language examinations to the Common European Framework of Reference for Languages (CEFR): A manual.* Strasbourg: The Council of Europe. Retrieved November 2016 from http://www.coe.int/t/dg4/linguistic/Source/ManualRevision-proofread-FINAL_en.pdf

Edwards Deming, W. (1993). *The new economics for industry, government, and education.* Boston, Ma: MIT Press.

Dudeney, G., & Hockly, N. (2014). *Going mobile: Teaching with hand-held devices.* Peaslake, UK: Delta Publishing.

Eaquals. (2014). *Eaquals self-assessment handbook.* London: Eaquals.

Eaquals. (2016a). *The Eaquals inspection scheme manual.* London: Eaquals.

Eaquals. (2016b). *The Eaquals inspection scheme manual and appendix: Guide to blended learning.* London: Eaquals.

Eaquals. (2004). *Eaquals quality seminar 2: Managing the teaching team.* London: Eaquals.

Everard, K. B., Morris, G., & Wilson, I. (2004). *Effective school management.* London: Paul Chapman Publishing.

Feigenbaum, A. V. (1983). *Total quality control, third edition.* New York, NY: McGraw-Hill Book Company.

Fowle, C. (2000). The skills transfer process from EFL teacher to educational manager. *ELT Management, 29,* 15–18.

Harmer, J. (2007). *The practice of English language teaching, fourth edition.* London: Pearson Education.

Heron, J. (2001). *Helping the client: A creative practical guide, fifth edition.* London: Sage.

Heyworth, F. (2013). Applications of quality management in language education. *Language Teaching, 46(3),* 281–315.

Howatt, A. P. R., & Widdowson, H. G. (2004). *A history of English language Teaching, second edition.* Oxford: Oxford University Press.

ISO. (2015). ISO 9001 *quality management systems – requirements.* Geneva: ISO.

Kerr, P. (2016, April). *The learner's own language.* Presentation at Eaquals International Conference, Lisbon, Portugal.

Kurtoglu-Hooten, N. (2016). From 'plodder' to 'creative': Feedback in teacher education. *ELT Journal, 70(1),* 39–47.

Labov, W. (1972). *Sociolinguistic Patterns.* Philadelphia: University of Pennsylvania Press.

Lewthwaite, J. (2006). *Managing people for the first time.* London: Thorogood Publishing Ltd.

Maingay, P. (1988). Observation for training, development or assessment. In T. Duff (Ed.), *Exploring in teacher training: Problems and issues* (pp. 118–131). Harlow, UK: Longman.

Malderez, A., & Wedell, M. (2007). *Teaching teachers: Processes and practices.* London: Continuum.

Mann, S. (2005). The language teacher's development. *Language Teaching, 38(2),* 103–118.

Martilla, J., & James, J. (1977). Importance-performance analysis. *Journal of Marketing, 41(1),* 77–79.

MET Project. (2012). *Asking students about teaching.* Seattle, WA: Bill & Melinda Gates Foundation. Retrieved December 2016 from http://k12education.gatesfoundation.org/wp-content/uploads/2015/12/Asking_Students_Practitioner_Brief.pdf

MET Project. (2013). *Ensuring fair and reliable measures of effective teaching.* Seattle, WA: Bill & Melinda Gates Foundation. Retrieved December 2016 from http://k12education.gatesfoundation.org/wp-content/uploads/2015/05/MET_Ensuring_Fair_and_Reliable_Measures_Practitioner_Brief.pdf

McCarthy, M. (2016). *The Cambridge guide to blended learning for language teaching.* Cambridge: Cambridge University Press.

Morrow, K. (2004). *Insights from the Common European Framework.* Oxford: Oxford University Press.

Munby, J. (1978). *Communicative syllabus design.* Cambridge: Cambridge University Press.

Oakland, J. (1988). *Total quality management.* London: Routledge.

Powell, G. (1999). How to avoid being a fly on the wall. *The Teacher Trainer, 13(1),* 3–5.

Soini, T., Pyhältö, K., & Pietarinen, J. (2010). Pupils' pedagogical well-being in comprehensive school—significant positive and negative school experiences of Finnish ninth graders. *European Journal of Psychology of Education, 25(2),* 207–221.

Randall, M., & Thornton, B. (2001). *Advising and supporting teachers.* Cambridge: Cambridge University Press.

Sharma, P. (2010). Blended learning. *ELT Journal, 64(4),* 456–458.

Sharma, P., Barrett, B., & Jones, F. (2014). *400 ideas for interactive whiteboards: Instant activities using technology.* London: Macmillan.

Tomlinson, B. (2011). *Materials development in language teaching.* Cambridge: Cambridge University Press.

Tomlinson, B. (2013). *Developing materials for language learning.* London: Bloomsbury.

Ur, P. (2012). *A course in English language teaching.* Cambridge: Cambridge University Press.

Walker, A., & White, G. (2013). *Technology enhanced language learning: Connecting theory and practice.* Oxford: Oxford University Press.

Wei, R. C., Darling-Hammond, L., Andree, A., Richardson, N., & Orphanos, S. (2009). *Professional learning in the learning profession: A status report on teacher development in the United States and abroad.* Dallas, TX: National Staff Development Council.

Wesker, A. (1960). *The Wesker trilogy.* New York: Random House.

White, R., Hockley, A., van der Horst Jansen, J., & Laughner, M. S. (2008). *From teacher to manager: Managing language teaching organizations.* Cambridge: Cambridge University Press.

INDEX

Page numbers annotated with 'g' and 'f' refer to glossary entries and figures respectively.

action plans 157–9
action research 60, 179g
adult education 106
agendas 42
appraisal 26, 91–7, 173f–4f, 179g
assessment for learning 114, 179g
assessment of learning 9–10, 52–4, 60, 107, 113–17, 179g
audio equipment 127–8
authoritarian vs. authoritative management style 30, 179g
Bailey, K. M. 74, 77
blended learning 8, 130–3, 179g
Blumberg, A. 45
Borg, S. 60
buddy system 27, 179g
bullying 93, 99, 100
buzz observations 138–9, 179g
BYOD approach (bring your own device) 128
CEN (Comité Européen de Normalisation) 151
CIPD (Chartered Institute of Personnel and Development) 91
classroom research 147, 180g
Common European Framework of Reference for Languages (CEFR) 103, 109–13, 117, 175f–7f, 180g
communication
 disciplinary process 25, 26, 37–40
 email 18, 22, 25, 40, 41, 42, 44–5
 grievances 25, 26, 38, 180g
 meetings 40–4
 videoconferencing 24, 41, 62
 webinars 62
 see also feedback
competence 70, 105–7, 114–15, 180g
complaints 139–41, 144–5
confidentiality 86, 97, 146
conflict management 34–40, 98–100, 139–41
continuing professional development (CPD) 10, 45–6, 57–72, 77–82, 180g
 assessment of needs 47–56, 77–80, 92–3, 96, 147
 costs 63
 recognition and rewards 70–1, 93
 in-service training (INSET) 10, 16, 60–2, 70, 71, 117, 181g

continuous assessment 116, 117
contracts 19, 25, 36, 38, 41, 61f, 71, 95, 98–100, 148
copyright 124–5
Council of Europe 111
course design 101–13
coursebooks 120–4
curriculum 9–10, 26, 101–13, 180g
data projectors 127
Deming, W Edwards 137
descriptor 180g
digital resources 123–4, 128, 129–30, 180g
disaffected teachers 35–6, 37–40
disciplinary process 25, 26, 37–40, 98–9
 see also grievances
documentation
 appraisal 26, 96–7, 173f–4f
 assessment and tests 117
 complaints and suggestions 139–41
 confidentiality 146
curriculum and syllabuses 102–3, 107–13, 182g
 disciplinary process 25, 26, 38, 98–9
 email 18, 22, 25, 40, 41, 42, 44–5
 grievances 25, 26, 38, 99–100
 induction and orientation 25–7
 meetings 42, 44
 recruitment 17–20, 25
 teacher development 54–5, 63, 69–70, 71
 teacher's logs 54, 63, 69–70, 75, 182g
 video recordings 21–2, 56, 64, 75, 80, 82, 86, 87–8
Eaquals 7, 8, 82–3, 102, 109–13, 114, 117, 125–7, 131, 138–9, 151–2, 154, 156–7, 180g
educational philosophy 109–10, 114
effectiveness 7, 52–4, 126f, 180g
email 18, 22, 25, 40, 41, 42, 44–5
equality 2, 36–7, 99, 126f, 153f
equipment (teaching equipment) 127–30
European Language Portfolio (ELP) 116, 180g
European Profiling Grid (EPG) 16, 70, 165f–71f, 180g
feedback
 complaints and suggestions 139–41, 144–5
 after lesson observation 79–80, 84, 86–8
 during recruitment process 25
 student feedback 7, 26, 53, 64, 84, 139–48
 see also performance management
 focus groups 7, 146, 180g

Fowle, C. 12
grievances 25, 26, 38, 99–100, 180g
gross misconduct 99
harassment 99
Heron, J. 49–51, 97
Heyworth, F. 136
ICT (information and communication technology) 41, 123–4, 128, 129–30, 145, 180g
'importance-performance' analysis 157–9
indicator 181g
induction 25–7, 181g
in-service training (INSET) 10, 16, 60–2, 70, 71, 117, 181g
inspectors 8, 82, 181g
institutional self-assessment 7, 8, 141, 149–60, 182g
intellectual property 124–5
interactive whiteboards (IWBs) 127, 181g
Internet 128, 129, 145–7
interventions 49–51
interviewing 22–5
ISO (International Organization for Standardization) 151, 152
James, J. 157–8
job descriptions 17–18, 23, 25, 37, 98, 138
Jonas, S. 45
Labov, W. 86
language course managers (LCMs) 8–13, 161–4, 181g
 authoritarian vs. authoritative styles 30, 179g
 communication skills 12, 40–6
 professional development 162–3, 181g
 team management skills 31–40, 45–6, 55–6, 163–4
learning management systems (LMSs) 128, 129–30, 145
learning resources 119–26, 127, 128, 129–30, 154–6
lesson observation 10–11, 53, 54, 73–88
 buzz observations 138–9, 179g
 checklists 78–9, 81
 consistency 88
 feedback 79–80, 84, 86–8
 observation schemes 63, 64, 73–4, 76, 84–8, 181g
 and quality assurance 82–4
 surprise observations 74, 83–4, 138
 and teacher development 77–82

unseen observations 74–5
lesson plans 85
Lewthwaite, J. 92
Maingay, P. 76–7, 82
Malderez, A. 66
Mann, S. 47, 62
Martilla, J. 157–8
meetings 40–4, 122
appraisal 26, 91–7, 173f–4f, 179g
complaints and suggestions 140–1
confidentiality 86, 97
disciplinary process 38–9
mentees 64–5, 67–8, 181g
mentoring 27, 55, 63, 64–8, 181g
mentors 65f, 67f, 181g
MET Project (Measures of Effective Teaching) 52–4, 139, 142–3
multimedia rooms 129
Munby, J. 104–5
needs analysis 49–51, 77–80, 92–3, 96, 147, 181g
students' needs 103–8
networks 129–30
observation schemes 63, 64, 73–4, 76, 84–8, 181g
observer's paradox 86
online/blended learning 8, 130–3, 179g
open enrolment courses 106, 107, 181g
PDCA cycle (plan-do-check-act) 137–8, 150–9
performance management 26, 90–100, 181g
appraisal 26, 91–7, 173f–4f, 179g
disciplinary process 25, 26, 37–40, 98–9
grievances 25, 26, 38, 99–100, 180g
person specifications 16–17, 21
photocopying 130
Pietarinen, J. 4
placement tests 107, 113–14
portfolios 116, 180g
Powell, G. 74–5
printing 130
professional development 10, 45–6, 57–72, 77–82, 181g, 182g
assessment of needs 47–56, 77–80, 92–3, 96, 147
costs 63
language course managers (LCMs) 162–3
recognition and rewards 70–1, 93
in-service training (INSET) 10, 16, 60–2, 70, 71, 117, 181g
professional learning 181g
Pyhältö, K. 4
quality 4–8, 36–7, 136–60
action plans 157–9
checklists 152–4
in curriculum and syllabus design 109–13

quality assurance 6–7, 26, 82–4, 115, 137, 138–48, 149–60, 181g
quality control 7, 136–8, 149, 182g
resources management 123, 126f
standards 6, 34f, 36–7, 82–4, 102, 109–17, 125–7, 138–9, 149–60, 182g
questionnaires 7, 142–8, 173f–4f
recording (video recording) 21–2, 56, 64, 75, 80, 82, 86
recruitment 15–27, 182g
induction 25–7, 181g
interviewing 22–5
legal requirements 19, 25
preparation stage 16–19
shortlisting 17, 20–2, 182g
reflection 55, 68, 79–80, 182g
reliability, of assessments 115
resources management 119–33, 154–6
copyright and intellectual property issues 124–5
finance and budgets 121, 122–3
selection of 120–2
teacher-developed resources 122–3, 124–5
teaching equipment 127–30
technical support 128–9
self-assessment
institutions 7, 8, 141, 149–60, 182g
students 116
teachers 24, 47, 54, 70
self-observation 58f, 75, 80, 182g
Sharma, P. 133
shortlisting 17, 20–2, 182g
Soini, T. 4
stakeholders 7, 26, 72, 129–30, 139–41, 147–8, 151, 156, 182g
standards 6, 34f, 36–7, 82–4, 102, 109–17, 125–7, 138–9, 149–60, 182g
students
feedback 7, 26, 53, 64, 84, 139–48
needs analysis 103–8
self-assessment 116
suggestions 139–41
surprise observations 74, 83–4, 138
surveys 142–8
syllabuses 102–3, 107–13, 182g
teacher development 10, 45–6, 57–72, 77–82, 182g
assessment of needs 47–56, 77–80, 92–3, 96, 147
costs 63
recognition and rewards 70–1, 93
in-service training (INSET) 10, 16, 60–2, 70, 71, 117, 181g
teacher trainers 182g
teachers 11–12
development of learning resources 122–3, 124–5

recruitment 15–27
self-assessment 24, 47, 54, 70
and team work 31–40, 45–6
teacher's logs 54, 63, 69–70, 75, 182g
teaching equipment 127–30
team management 31–40, 55–6, 59–62, 163–4
team teaching 63
tests 9–10, 53, 60, 103, 107, 113–16
time management 10–11
total quality management (TQM) 136–8, 149, 182g
unseen observations 74–5
Ur, P. 55
validity, of assessments 115, 117
values 109–10, 114
video recordings 21–2, 56, 64, 75, 80, 82, 86, 87–8
videoconferencing 24, 41, 62
washback effect 116, 182g
webinars 62
Wedell, M. 66
Wei, R. C. 59
Wesker, A. 116
White, R. 91